GLOSSARY-INDEX
FOR
"A COURSE IN MIRACLES"

KENNETH WAPNICK, Ph.D.

Coleman Graphics
99 Milbar Blvd.
Farmingdale, N.Y. 11735

ISBN #0942494-26-1

Printed in the United States of America by
Coleman Graphics
99 Milbar Blvd.
Farmingdale, N.Y. 11735

CONTENTS

INTRODUCTION

Unlike most thought systems, *A Course in Miracles* does not proceed in a truly linear fashion with its theoretical structure built upon increasingly complex ideas. Rather, the Course's development is more circular with its themes treated symphonically: introduced, set aside, reintroduced and developed. This results in an interlocking matrix in which every part is integral and essential to the whole, while implicitly containing that whole within itself.

This structure establishes a *process* of learning instead of merely setting forth a theoretical system. The process resembles the ascent up a spiral staircase. The reader is led in a circular pattern, each revolution leading higher until the top of the spiral is reached, which opens unto God. Thus, the same material consistently recurs, both within the Course as a thought system as well as in learning opportunities in our personal lives. Each revolution, as it were, leads us closer to our spiritual goal. The last two paragraphs on page 13 in the text particularly emphasize this cumulative impact of the Course's learning process.

Through careful study of the text, along with the daily practice that the workbook provides, the student is gradually prepared for the deeper experiences of God towards which the Course points. Intellectual mastery of its thought system will not suffice to bring about the perceptual and experiential transformation that is the Course's aim.

This Glossary-Index was prepared as a guide for students of *A Course in Miracles.* It is not a substitute for working through the material itself. Rather, it is intended as an aid in studying and understanding the Course's thought system. This book is divided into three sections. The first briefly summarizes the Course's theory, presenting the interrelationships among the more important terms to be defined. These words are in bold face.

Following this summary is an alphabetical listing of these and additional terms, in four divisions: One-mindedness, wrong-mindedness, right-mindedness, and related terms.

The second section presents all the terms in alphabetical order. Each is defined as it is used in the Course. Several words, especially those pertaining to One-mindedness, have no precise meaning in this world and their definitions can only be approximated here. As the Course says: ". . . words are but symbols of symbols. They are thus twice removed from reality" (manual, p. 51). It should be noted that many of the terms have different meanings or connotations outside the Course, and these should not be confused with the Course's usage. Moreover, some words have differing uses in the Course itself, reflecting knowledge or perception (e.g., *extension*), right- or wrong-mindedness (e.g., *denial*).

Following the definition is a selected and subheaded index of the principal pages in the text, workbook and manual where the terms are most meaningfully discussed. The most important of these references are in bold type. Unlike a concordance, not every reference for a term is noted. In general there is only a single subheading for each page reference; however, multiple listings have been included when that subheading is particularly important, or where there are separate references on a page. Occasionally a term is referenced when it is *described*, though the term itself is not mentioned; e.g., the reference on page 43 in the manual for *projection*, subheaded under *guilt*. The capitalization used in the Course is followed in this book. Thus, the Persons of the Trinity — God, Christ (Son of God), Holy Spirit — are always capitalized, as are all pronouns referring back to Them. Pronouns referring to the Son of God in his separated state are in lower case. Words that directly relate to the Trinity, such as *Love, Will, Heaven*, etc., are capitalized, though their pronouns are not.

The final section is an index of scriptural references in the Course, all taken from the King James Version, the translation used by the Course. The first part lists these references sequentially as they are found in the three books. The second lists them as they are found sequentially in the Bible. Many of the references are found in more than one book of the Bible, but only the more important or widely known of these have been cross-referenced.

The key that is followed in the index is: T = text; W = workbook; m = manual. The letter "f" after a page means the next following page is included in the reference; e.g., T119f refers to pages 119 and 120 in the text. When a new section is begun in the middle of a page the listings are separated; e.g., the subheading *Holy Spirit* under *justice:* T497-501,501f. The letters "T" and "B" following each line reference refer to "top" and "bottom," respectively; e.g., line 10T refers to the tenth line from the top; line 15B refers to the fifteenth line from the bottom.

Finally, I would like to express my gratitude and appreciation to Esther Adam, Joan Adam, Sr. Joan Metzner, Joan Pantesco, Sharon Reis, my wife Gloria, and countless others who have helped in the preparation of the manuscript; and to the Foundation for Inner Peace, publishers of *A Course In Miracles,* for permission to publish this Glossary-Index.

I. THEORY

I. Theory

The Course distinguishes two worlds: God and the ego, knowledge and perception, truth and illusion. Strictly speaking, every aspect of the post-separation world of perception reflects the ego. However, the Course further subdivides the world of perception into wrong- and right-mindedness. Within this framework the Course almost always uses the word "ego" to denote wrong-mindedness, while right-mindedness is the domain of the Holy Spirit, teaching forgiveness as the correction for the ego. Thus, we can speak of three thought systems: **One-mindedness,** which belongs to knowledge, and **wrong-** and **right-mindedness** which reflect the world of perception. Our discussion will follow this tri-partite view of mind.

The accompanying table summarizes the Course's description of the mind. It should be examined in conjunction with the following references from the Course which deal with the relationship of spirit to mind, spirit to ego, and the three levels of mind:

> text   : p. 10 - par. 4
>   p. 37 - par. 3 through p. 39 - top
>   p. 48 - pars. 1,2
>   p. 122 - pars. 2,3, through p. 123, par. 2
>
> workbook: p. 167 - pars. 3,4,5
> manual : pp. 75f

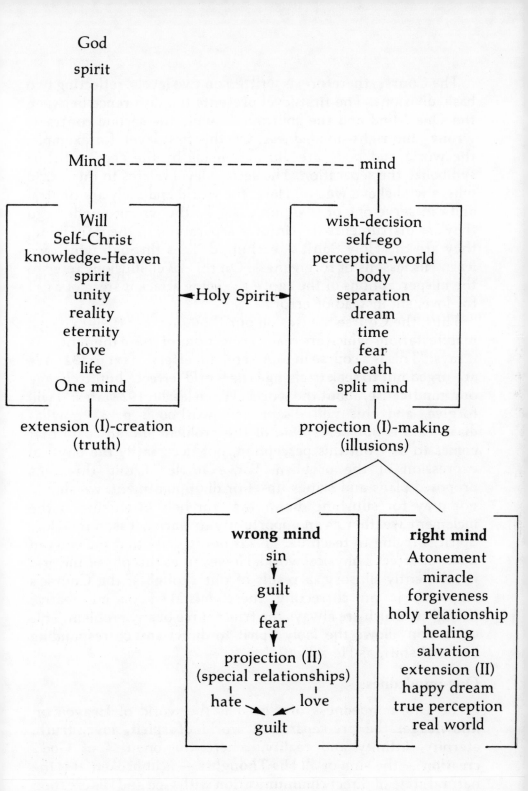

God
spirit

Mind ─ ─ ─ ─ ─ ─ ─ ─ ─ ─ ─ ─ ─ ─ ─ mind

Will
Self-Christ
knowledge-Heaven
spirit
unity
reality
eternity
love
life
One mind

◄Holy Spirit►

wish-decision
self-ego
perception-world
body
separation
dream
time
fear
death
split mind

extension (I)-creation
(truth)

projection (I)-making
(illusions)

wrong mind
sin
↓
guilt
↓
fear
↓
projection (II)
(special relationships)
hate ↘   ↙ love
guilt

right mind
Atonement
miracle
forgiveness
holy relationship
healing
salvation
extension (II)
happy dream
true perception
real world

3

The Course, therefore, is written on two levels, reflecting two basic divisions. The first level presents the difference between the One Mind and the split mind, while the second contrasts wrong- and right-mindedness. On this first level, for example, the world and body are illusions made by the ego, and thus symbolize the separation. The second level relates to this world where we believe we are. Here, the world and body are neutral and can serve one of two purposes. To the wrong-minded ego they are instruments to reinforce separation; to the right mind, they are the Holy Spirit's teaching devices through which we learn His lessons of forgiveness. On this level, illusions refer to the misperceptions of the ego; e.g., seeing attack instead of a call for love, sin instead of error.

Thus, the Course focuses on our thoughts, not their external manifestations which are really projections of these thoughts. As it says: "This is a course in cause and not effect" (text p. 432). We are urged not to seek to change the world (**effect**), but to change our mind (**cause**) about the world . When lesson 193 states: "I will forgive, and this will disappear" (workbook p. 359), what disappears is our perception of the problem and any pain that comes to us from this perception, not necessarily the physical expression of the problem. For example, if rain threatens proposed plans and brings upset or disappointment, we should not pray for sunshine, but rather for help in looking at the inclement weather as an opportunity to learn a lesson the Holy Spirit is trying to teach us. This is not to deny that the ego can make or affect a physical world. However, as this physical world is inherently illusory, a result of our thoughts, the Course's emphasis is on correcting these mistaken or miscreative thoughts, which are always the true source of any problem. This correction allows the Holy Spirit to direct any corresponding external shift, as He sees fit.

One-mindedness

The One-mindedness of Christ is the world of **Heaven** or **knowledge**: the pre-separation world of **spirit, love,** truth, eternity, infinity and reality, where the oneness of God's **creation** — the sum of all His **Thoughts** — is unbroken. It is the natural state of direct **communication** with God and His creation that existed before the mind of God's Son thought of separation. In this state the perfect unity of the **Trinity** is maintained.

The Trinity consists of: 1) **God,** the **Father;** 2) His **Son, Christ,** our true **Self;** and 3) the **Holy Spirit,** the **Voice for God.** Included in the Second Person of the Trinity are our **creations,** the extensions of our Self or spirit. The Second Person of the Trinity is not exclusively identified with **Jesus,** who is part of Christ, as we all are.

Wrong-mindedness

The ego consists of three fundamental concepts: **sin:** the belief that we have separated ourselves from God; **guilt:** the experience of having sinned, of having done something wrong by attacking God; and **fear:** believing we have done something wrong, we inevitably believe we shall be punished for our sin, and therefore fear the punishment from God our guilt tells us we deserve.

To ensure its survival the ego continually attracts guilt to itself, since guilt proves sin's reality and it is sin that gave the ego birth. Once it has established guilt as real the ego teaches us never to approach or even look at it, for it says we would either be destroyed by an angry, vengeful God intent on punishing us for our sin against Him, or else annihilated in the oblivion of our own nothingness. This fear keeps the guilt and sin intact, for without seeing them as decisions of our mind we can never change our belief in them.

Left with the anxiety and terror brought on by the fear of God, our only recourse is to turn to the ego for help, since God has become our enemy. The ego's plan of salvation from guilt has two parts: the first is **denial,** wherein we push our guilt out of awareness, hoping that by not seeing the problem it will not be there. Secondly, after the guilt is denied, we project it out from us onto another, **magically** hoping to be free from the guilt by unconsciously placing it outside ourselves.

Projection has two principal forms: **special hate** and **special love relationships.** In special hate relationships our self-hatred or guilt is transferred onto others, making them responsible for the misery we feel. Our **anger** or **attack** attempts to justify the projection, reinforcing others' guilt for the sins we projected from ourselves. Special love relationships have the same goal of projecting guilt, though the form differs greatly. Our guilt teaches we are empty, unfulfilled, incomplete and needful, all aspects of the **scarcity principle.** Believing this lack can never be corrected, we seek outside ourselves for those people who can complete us. Special love, thus, takes this form: I have certain special needs that God cannot meet, but you, a special person with special attributes, can meet them for me. When you do I shall love you. If you do not, my "love" will turn to hate.

The ego's world becomes divided into enemies (special hate) or savior-**idols** (special love), and the true Identity of Christ in others is obscured. **Judgment,** always based on the past, rather than acceptance in the present is the ego's guiding principle. Through special relationships the ego sustains its existence by maintaining guilt, since using others to meet our needs constitutes an attack, and attack in any form reinforces guilt. This sets into motion the guilt-attack cycle, wherein the greater our guilt, the greater the need to project it by attacking others through special relationships, which merely adds to the guilt, increasing the need to project it.

The ego's wrong-mindedness is a **dream** of **separation,** most clearly expressed in the physical **world.** The **body's** existence is one of **sickness, suffering** and **death,** which witness to the seeming reality of the body as opposed to spirit, which can never suffer pain, or die. **Crucifixion** is the Course's symbol of the ego, representing the belief in attack and **sacrifice,** where one's gain depends on another's loss. All aspects of the separated world are **illusions,** since what is of God can never be separate from Him, and what seems separate from God cannot be real.

Right-mindedness

God's **Answer** to the separation is the Holy Spirit, and His plan to undo the ego is called the **Atonement.** The Course employs many terms that reflect the Holy Spirit's plan, and each is a virtual synonym for the other. They include: **miracle, forgiveness, salvation, healing, real world, true perception, vision, face of Christ, reason, justice, holy instant, holy relationship, function, happy dream, Second Coming, Word of God, Last (Final) Judgment, resurrection,** redemption, correction, awakening and undoing.

These terms, belonging to the separated world of perception, refer to the process (miracle) that corrects our misperceptions, shifting from hearing the ego's voice of sin, guilt and fear, to the Holy Spirit's Voice of forgiveness. In this way, special or unholy relationships become holy. Without these relationships we would have no way of being freed from the guilt the ego has taught us to bury through denial and retain through projection. The Holy Spirit turns the tables on the ego by changing *its* purpose for projection into an opportunity to see this denied guilt in another, allowing us finally to change our mind about it.

While the practice of forgiveness, or undoing guilt, is usually a complex and long-term one, it can be understood essentially as a three step process (see, e.g., page 83 in the text, and pages 34, 118 and 365 in the workbook). The first step reverses the projection as we realize that the guilt is not in another but in ourselves. Second, now that the guilt has been brought to our attention and we recognize that its source is in us, we undo this decision by choosing to see ourselves as guiltless Sons of God, rather than guilty sons of the ego. These two steps are our responsibility; the final one is the Holy Spirit's, Who is able to take the guilt from us now that we have released it to Him. Using the workbook as our guide, we become trained over time to hear His Voice, learning that "All things are lessons (in forgiveness) God would have me learn" (workbook, p. 357).

When our guilt is finally undone, right-mindedness having corrected wrong-mindedness, the **bridge** to the real world is complete. The **memory of God** dawns within our mind, as all interferences to it have been removed and we see the face of Christ in all people. This world of illusion and separation ends as God takes the **last step,** reaching down and lifting us unto Himself. Restored to the One-mindedness of Christ, "we are home where . . . (God) would have us be" (text, p. 622).

One-mindedness

abundance
Christ
communication
communion
creation
creations
extension
God
Great Rays
Heaven (Kingdom of God, Heaven)
Holy Spirit (Answer, Voice for God)
knowledge
laws of God
Love
Mind of God
Name of God
One-mindedness
Self
Son of God
spirit
Thoughts of God
Trinity
Will of God

Wrong-mindedness

attack (anger)

body

crucifixion

death

defenses

denial

devil

dissociation

dream

ego

fear

gap

guilt

hell

idol

illusion

judgment

magic

perception

projection

sacrifice

scarcity principle

separation

sickness

sin

special relationship

suffering

temptation

time

world

wrong-mindedness

Right-mindedness

accepting the Atonement
a little willingness
Atonement
face of Christ
faith
forgiveness
free will
free will — A
function
grace
gratitude
happy dream
healing
holy instant
holy relationship
innocence
invulnerability

justice
Last (Final) Judgment
last step
memory of God
miracle
prayer
real world
reason
resurrection
revelation
right-mindedness
salvation
Second Coming
teacher of God
true perception
vision
Word of God

Related Terms

A Course in Miracles
"bringing darkness (illusions)
    to the light (truth)"
cause/effect
Christmas
decision
Easter
form/content
gift
giving/receiving
having/being
humility/arrogance
"I am as God created me"

"ideas leave not their source"
Jesus
make/create
means/end
mind
"no order of difficulty in
    miracles"
"periods of unsettling"
questions
"senseless musings"
teaching/learning
wish/will

Symbols
altar
angels
bridge
lilies
song of Heaven
star
thorns
toys
war

II. GLOSSARY-INDEX

abundance

Heaven's principle that contrasts with the ego's belief in scarcity; God's Son can never lack anything or be in need, since God's gifts, given eternally in creation, are always with him.

(Note — since abundance and scarcity are usually discussed together, *scarcity* and related ego concepts are not cross-referenced below.)

charity T52

creation T517

extension T119,**120**

God T**56**,**120**,**555**

grandeur T166

innocence T33

real world W408

Sonship T10; W307

truth T9

accepting the Atonement

accepting the unreality of sin and guilt, sickness and death, by following the specific curriculum in forgiveness established for us by the Holy Spirit; this is our one responsibility, our function in the Atonement.

A Course in Miracles

the Course frequently refers to itself; its goal is not love or God, but the undoing, through forgiveness, of the interferences of guilt and fear that prevent our acceptance of Him; its primary focus, therefore, is on the ego and its undoing, rather than on Christ or spirit.

a little willingness

our little willingness, joined with the Holy Spirit, is all the Atonement requires; our ego seems to make the undoing of guilt impossible, but the willingness to forgive allows the Holy Spirit to undo it for us.

Course T417,464

decision T25

forgiveness T572,616f

holy instant T288,335,**354-56**

Holy Spirit T26,145,183,291,316,328,**357f,497**

miracle T158,557

real world T195,237,323

salvation T516; W364

Second Coming W439

vision T299f, 441

16

altar

w-m: used rarely as symbol of the ego's presence.

r-m: symbol of God's presence in us; the meeting-place of God and His Son; not an external structure, but an attitude or devotion.

Atonement T18f,34,**207**,244

belief T102

Christ T187,213

church T86

defilement T18,22f,207

ego T238,296; W457

forgiveness T488,**510**; W346

gifts T270; W183

God T173,246,288; W72,346

holiness T287,579

holy relationship T374; W334

Holy Spirit T70,114,269,283f

lilies/thorns **T397-99**

Self T186; W444

Son of God T**36**,269,579; W447; M82

special relationships ... T319

true perception T36,**213**; M82

angels

extensions of God's Thought; symbol of the light and protection
of God that always surrounds us.

anger
(see: attack)

Answer
(see: Holy Spirit)

Atonement

the Holy Spirit's plan of correction to undo the ego and heal the belief in separation; it came into being with the creation of the Holy Spirit after the separation, and will be completed when every separated Son has fulfilled his part in the Atonement by total forgiveness.

attack

the attempt to justify the projection of guilt onto others, demonstrating their sinfulness and guilt so that we may feel free of it; because attack is always a projection of responsibility for the separation, it is never justified; also used to denote the sin of separation against God, for which we believe God will attack us in return.

(Note — attack and anger are used virtually synonymously.)

body	T85,140-43,**143-45**,567; W122f,297f
Christ	T187,491
defenses	W245,**277f**,318
dream	T350f,569
ego	T117,147,206,223,387; W120
fear	T84,451; W318f,364f; M42-44
forgiveness	T460f,**593f**; W355f
God	T187,491f; W122f
guilt	T295-97,460f; M**45**
Holy Spirit	T200-2; M68
idol	T588f
injustice	T**522-24**,525
invulnerability	T92,209f; W40
Jesus	T85-87
judgment	W467; M11
laws of chaos	T455-59
love	T202; W114,349; M21
magic	M**42-44**,45
mind	T206f,472; W297f
miracle	T462f; W137f
peace	M49
projection	T**84**,85-88,89,119; W33,**364f**
sacrifice	T296,302f,504
sickness	T525f,528,560

body

level I: the embodiment of the ego; the thought of separation projected by the mind into form; the seeming witness to the reality of the separation; includes both our physical bodies as well as our personalities.

level II: the body is inherently neutral, neither "good" or "evil"; its purpose is given it by the mind.

w-m: the body is the symbol of guilt and attack.

r-m: the body is the instrument of salvation, the means of teaching and learning forgiveness whereby the ego's guilt is undone.

Christ T482f

dream T543f; W415

ego T60,93,300,364f,409; W372

fear T422; W297f

forgiveness T526-28; W355; M81

guilt T359f,368,384,387

healing T111,146,371f,561f; W246,415

holy instant T300f

Holy Spirit T140-43,301,407f; W155,372f

instrument of salvation .. T145f,473-75; W282,322,401,436, 439,469,471; M30f,69,86

mind T20,359-62,423,480,559f; W245f

perception T38

projection T552; W298

sacrifice T422f,504f

separation T371f,560,563f

sickness T144-46; W251-53; M16f

sin T606f; W409

special relationships ... T321,331,407-9,472,479

body (cont'd)

bridge

symbol for the transition from perception to knowledge; thus it is equated variously with the Holy Spirit, the real world, and God's last step; it is used alternately to denote the actual shift from perception to knowledge, as well as the shift from false to true perception and the real world.

creations T313,315
forgiveness W243; M79
God T314-17,320,550
Holy Spirit T72,90,316; W427
peace W375
real world T321-23,328f,513
time/eternity T17,316f,328f

bringing darkness (illusions) to the light (truth)

the process of undoing denial, expressing the decision to bring our guilt to the light of the Holy Spirit to be forgiven, rather than fearfully keeping it in the darkness of our unconscious minds; living in illusions brings sickness and pain, bringing them to truth is healing and salvation.

Atonement **T270f**

Christ T620; W421

Christ's vision W440,442

conflict T454; W459

death T336; M64

dissociation **T266-68**

error T16; W189

fear **T264-66**; W182

forgiveness T449; W242f,420,457; M65,82

guilt T225,295

healing T159; W250,252,264; M19

Heaven/hell W258

holy instant T418,**533-35**; W395

holy relationship T354

Holy Spirit T227,269,276f,**328**,367,545f; W427

sin T375f,411

special relationships ... T314

teachers of God M18

cause/effect

cause and effect are mutually dependent, since the existence of one determines the existence of the other; moreover, if something is not a cause it cannot exist, since all being has effects.

knowledge: God is the only *Cause*, and His Son is His *Effect*.

perception: the sin of separation is the *cause* of the dream of suffering and death, which is sin's *effect*; forgiveness undoes sin by showing others that their "sins" against us have had no effect; not having effects, sin cannot be a cause and therefore cannot exist.

attack T209f,523

dream T473,**539-42,551-53,553-55**,555-57

ego T312

fear T188,258,519f; M44

forgiveness T157f,435,**528f**

God T28,151,256,**550**

guilt T**256**,547; W287

magic M40

miracle T24,517,538,549,552f,598

sickness T514f,551,560; W250f

sin T258,**527**; W179

Son of God T420,550; W454

thoughts T27,415; W26f,28,30

time T548

world T539-42,**544-46**; W34f,351f

Christ

the Second Person of the Trinity; the one Son of God or totality of the Sonship; the Self That God created by extension of His spirit; though Christ creates as does His Father, He is not the Father since God created Christ, but Christ did not create God.

(Note — Christ is not to be equated exclusively with Jesus.)

anti-Christ T575-77

Atonement T207

attack T491

birth W441,443

body T476-78,**482f**; W299

completion **T473-75**

creation T58

forgiveness T444f; W292,294,356

Friend T394,396f

God T152,**187,213,**622

guilt T221,234

healing T197f,203

holy relationship T437f,441,604f

Holy Spirit T233,483

Jesus M**83f**,85

Mind T68,482; M75

Presence T191,521f,522-24; W290

rebirth T441,605; W331-33,356; M87

risen Christ T192,396f,522

Second Coming T58; W439

Self T292; W**421**

Son of God T187,**197**

strength T620; W103

time of Christ T302,304,306

touch T235; W309f

vision T212f,233,241; W442

Christmas

the holiday commemorating the birth of Jesus; used as a symbol for the rebirth of Christ in ourselves: the "time of Christ."

Jesus T286,**301f**,305f
time of Christ T301f,**304-6**

communication

knowledge: synonymous with creation, an expression of our relationship to God which can be likened to a flow of spirit and love; only spirit can communicate, unlike the ego, which is separate by nature.

perception: we experience communication in our right mind through the Holy Spirit, sharing His Love with others.

Atonement T263

body T**140-43**,300f; W122; M65

creation T**63f**,150

forgiveness T**297f**

God/Son T259,269; W229,335

holy instant T289,294

Holy Spirit T4,**97**,261f,265f,274

mind T**111**,289,305f,405

miracle T20f

psychic powers M59

revelation T4,64

separation T70,95,265

spirit T48,63

symbols T597; W337

communion

the joining of Father, Son and Holy Spirit, Whose union seemed broken by the separation; awareness of this union is restored to us through the holy relationship.

body T140,**384**

communication T97

fear T8

holy relationship/Jesus .. T383,**385f**

Holy Spirit T74,114,384

miracle T9,41

creation

the extension of God's being or spirit, the Cause, that resulted in His Son, the Effect; described as the First Coming of Christ; it is the Son's function in Heaven to create, as God created Him.

see: *creations*

(Note — creation exists only at the level of knowledge, and is not equivalent to creation or creativity as known in the world of perception.)

communication	**T63f**
extension	**T14**,90,104f,333,377,462
First Coming	T58,158
forgiveness	W355
Holy Spirit	T68,312
knowledge	T270
laws of God	T174
Mind of God	T64,177,495
separation	T241,559
sharing	T64,176
Son of God	**T550**; **W451**
Will of God	T130f
Word of God	W424

creations

the extensions of our spirit; the effects of our creating, analogous to the creation when God created His Son by extending Himself; creation occurs continuously in Heaven, independent of the Son's lack of awareness of it in this world.

see: *creation*

Atonement T77
creation T168f,270,315,**550**; W237,451
dissociation T63,162
extension T**14,104f**,180f,286
God T124,162f,242,298,420,468; W454
forgiveness T510,572f
Holy Spirit T68,131,300,**312**
joy T113,117,489
spirit T54,**122f**
Trinity T**138f**

crucifixion

a symbol of the ego's attack on God and therefore on His Son, witnessing to the "reality" of suffering, sacrifice and death which the world seems to manifest; it also refers to the crucifixion of Jesus, an extreme example that taught that our true identity of love can never be destroyed, for death has no power over life.

(Note — since crucifixion and resurrection are usually discussed together, *resurrection* is not cross-referenced below.)

decision T**192-94**,255

ego T225,264

faithlessness T345

forgiveness T**396**,397-99,518

Jesus T32,**84-88**,193f,396; W322

message T47,87

projection T85-87; W364

sacrifice T**32f,525-27**

suffering T395; W457

world T220

death

w-m: the final witness to the seeming reality of the body and the separation from our Creator Who is Life; it is seen as the ultimate punishment for our sin of separation.

r-m: the quiet laying down of the body after it has fulfilled its purpose as a teaching device.

attack T228; W298

attraction T**388-91**,392

body T96f,389f,574; W435

decision T46,388; W274; M16

dream T571; M77

ego T216f,**280f**,387f

God T572f; W122,**302f**; M49f,**63f**,84

Holy Spirit T538f; M31

Jesus T97,217; M55

mind **W311f**

resurrection M65

separation M47

sin T383,494,498; W179

special relationship T335f, 474

decision

the last remaining freedom as prisoner of this world is our power to decide; while unknown in Heaven, decision is necessary here as it was our decision to be separate that must be corrected; this is accomplished by choosing the Holy Spirit instead of the ego, right-mindedness instead of wrong-mindedness.

body	T476f,614
Christ	T619f
death	T388; W274
dissociation	T169f
dreams/awakening	T541f,568f
forgiveness	W460
healing	T182f
Heaven/hell	W**257-59**,352; M51
holiness	T413,415
Holy Spirit	T70,**83,255-59,260**,285f,**418**
imprisonment/freedom	T215,430
Jesus	T39,287
joy	T82f,489; W351f
littleness/magnitude	T285f
mind	T53,114
miracle	T256,598; W137f
projection/extension	**T215f**
real world/world	T509; W229
right-/wrong-mindedness	M75
rules	**T581-84**
sickness	W**250f**; M**16-18**,53
sin/error	T489
time	T intro.; M4
truth/illusions	T332,603; W**239-41,274f**,284f, 339f
vision	T405; W31,42,43
world	T607-9

defenses

w-m: the devices we use to "protect" ourselves from our guilt, fear and seeming attacks of others, the most important defenses being denial and projection; by their very nature defenses do what they would defend, as they reinforce the belief in our own vulnerability which merely increases our fear and belief that we need defense.

r-m: defenses are reinterpreted as the means to free us from fear; e.g., denial denies "the denial of truth," and projecting our guilt becomes the means of forgiving it.

Atonement T16f,17f

attack T93,461; W245f,277,318f; M49

crucifixion T32

defenselessness W277-80,332f; M12f

denial T16,118

fear T202

holy instant T335

Holy Spirit T268

illusion T445-47; W278

invulnerability T267f; M39

planning W246-49

sickness W250-53

sin T399,446

special relationships ... T334f

theology M73

time W252,329

denial

w-m: avoiding guilt by pushing the decision that made it out of awareness, rendering it inaccessible to correction or Atonement; roughly equivalent to repression.

r-m: used to deny error and affirm truth.

body	T20,372,387
defenses	W250f
ego	T59f,115
fear	T202,224
Holy Spirit	T118,213
mind	T118
projection	T16,121,206,224,387,539-42; M43
right mind/miracle worker	T16,203f
separation	W139; M43
vision	T232; W154

devil

a projection of the ego, which attempts to deny responsibility for our sin and guilt by projecting it onto an external agent.

dissociation

an ego defense that separates spirit from ego, splitting off what seems fearful, which merely reinforces the fear that is the ego's goal; the ego's attempt to separate two conflicting thought systems and keep them both in our minds, so that *its* thought system is safe from undoing.

creations T63

ego/fear T280f

ego/spirit T61f

knowledge T169f,427

mind W167

projection T88f,215

separation T88,267

truth T136

dream

the post-separation state in which the Son of God dreams a world of sin, guilt and fear, believing this to be reality and Heaven a dream; the Son, being the dreamer, is the *cause* of the world which is the *effect*, although this relationship between cause and effect appears reversed in this world, as we seem to be the effect or victim of the world; occasionally used to denote sleeping dreams, although there is no real difference between them and waking dreams for both are part of the illusory world of perception.

see: *happy dream*

attack	T431,539-42
body	T543-45; W415
cause/effect	T**539-43,543-45,551-53**,553-55,555f
crucifixion	T194
darkness	T232,352-54
death	T571; M63f
ego	T48,94; M77
fear	T558,569; W458
form/content	T351,568f; W339
God	T94
idol	T574,577f
judgment	T577-79
separation	T14f,552
sickness	T551-53,553-55,555-57; W263
sin	M83
sleeping dreams	T15,169,**350-52**
special relationships	T471
teacher of God	M31
time	W312

Easter

the holiday commemorating the resurrection of Jesus; since the resurrection transcended the ego by overcoming death, Easter is used as a symbol for the offering and acceptance of redemption or ego transcendence through forgiveness.

forgiveness T396;398f; W273

Jesus T396f

resurrection T394f

salvation T397; W249

ego

the belief in the reality of the separated or false self, made as substitute for the Self Which God created; the thought of separation that gives rise to sin, guilt and fear, and a thought system based on attack to protect itself; the part of the mind that believes it is separate from the Mind of Christ; this split mind has two parts: wrong- and right-mindedness; *ego* is almost always used to denote "wrong-mindedness," but can include "right-mindedness," the part of the ego that can learn.

(Note — *ego* is not to be equated with the "ego" of psychoanalysis, but can be roughly equated with the entire psyche, of which the psychoanalytic "ego" is a part.)

attack	T114-17,164,165f,190f
authority problem/autonomy	T43,**51-53**,179,**188-90**; W122
belief	T61,77,**121f**
body	T52f,**59-61**,93; W372
death/hell	**T280f**
fear	T115,188-90,302
guilt	T77f,242-44,295-97; W240
Holy Spirit	T72f,92f; W109f
illusions	T452f; W21; M77f
Jesus	T51
judgment	T80,273f; W271
love	T207f
plan of salvation	T157,**223**; W120f,122f
projection	T89,119f,120f,**223f**
separation	T37,55; W**457**
sickness	T144f,171f
sin	T375f,423f
special relationships	T**295-97**,337f
spirit	T47,48-51,54f
time	T72f,229f,280f
wish/will	T124f; W125
world	T74,400
wrong-mindedness	T56; M75

extension

knowledge: the ongoing process of creation, wherein spirit flows from itself.

perception: extending the Holy Spirit or Christ's vision in the form of forgiveness or peace; the Holy Spirit's use of the law of mind, contrasted with the ego's projection.

creating T14f,**105**,117,138f,180f,286; W451

creation T90,462

forgiveness T449,568

giving W345f

holy relationship T435f

Holy Spirit T91,120,**153**

law of mind T**106f,120**,215

mind T90f,142

miracle T309,**535**,549

peace T379,386; W51

projection T14f,106,179

spirit **T122f**

vision W45,**47**,55,293

Will of God T131f; W133,456

face of Christ

symbol of forgiveness; the face of innocence seen in another when we look through Christ's vision, free from our projections of guilt; thus it is the extension onto others of the guiltlessness we see in ourselves, independent of what our physical eyes see.

(Note — not to be confused with the face of Jesus.)

fear	T391
forgiveness	T403f; W**213**,370,**421**; M15,65, 79f
healing	M54
holy instant	T405f, 536; W316
Holy Spirit	W272; M85
idol	T576
memory of God	T592; W213; M83
sin	T**444**,510,521
vision/true perception	T405,476,**617-19**; W420; M66, 81f

faith

the expression of where we choose to place our trust; we are free to have faith in the ego or the Holy Spirit, in the illusion of sin in others or in the truth of their holiness as Sons of God.

belief T243,421-23,427

body T386,422f; W154f

faithlessness T343f,**371-74**,562

healing T373f

holy instant T345

holy relationship T338,**343f**,373f,393

Holy Spirit T342,357,373f,419; W412

justice T497

love/illusion W79

miracle T175; W463

problem solving T342f

sin T419,421-23

sinlessness **W329f**

teacher of God M14

truth/illusion T372

vision **T421-23**

fear

the emotion of the ego, contrasted with love, the emotion given us by God; fear originates in the expected punishment for our sins, which our guilt demands; the resulting terror over what we believe we deserve leads us to defend ourselves by attacking others, which merely reinforces our sense of vulnerability and fear, establishing a vicious circle of fear and defense.

Atonement T74

attack T84,85,**119**; W114,297f; M43

authority problem/ego autonomy .. T15,38,43f,45,49f

body T387,422; W297f

death T46,280f,389-91; M63f

defenses W**245,318**

dissociation T169f

dreams T351

ego T50,72,77,115,**188-90**,280f

forgiveness T157,**393**

God T**225-27**,391f,393,449,456, 461; W182,319,364f; M43

guilt T**382**,437,594; M67

healing T21-23,535

illusion T315,318,320,459

judgment T596

love T12,**201f**,230f,302f,347; W295

mind T**24-27**

punishment T77,376,460

sin T376,520; W414

sinlessness T**423-25**

special relationships T315,466

thoughts T27f; W461

world T367f; W21,231,402,403

forgiveness

our special function that shifts perception of another as "enemy" (special hate) or "savior-idol" (special love) to brother or friend, removing all projections of guilt from him; the expression of the miracle or vision of Christ, that sees all people united in the Sonship of God, looking beyond the seeming differences that reflect separation; thus, perceiving sin makes true forgiveness impossible; forgiveness recognizes that what we thought was done to us we truly did to ourselves, for only we can deprive ourselves of the peace of God; therefore, we forgive others for what they have *not* done to us, not for what they did.

Atonement T156f

attack W137f,369-71

ego T157

face of Christ W213; M15,**79f**

function T260,**492-94**; W103,344,355,374

God T326,470f,585f; W73

guilt M81f

happy dream T542f,579f,590; W263,294,369,412

healing T528-31; W254-56; M53f

holy relationship T393-95,448-50,491f

Holy Spirit T**157f**,488; W391

illusions T325f,568; W369f; M79

invulnerability T**256**; W456

love W344

miracles W137f

perception T41; W460

prayer T40

real world T**328-30, 368-70**,452,590-92,593f; W130f,408,420,433

salvation W174f,213-15

sin T**593-95**; W210-12,222f,**242-44**,391

special relationships ... T330-33,**470f**

forgiveness (cont'd)

form/content

the world's multitude of forms conceals the simplicity of their content: truth or illusion; the ego attempts to convince us our problems are on the level of form, so that their underlying content, fear, escapes notice and correction; the Holy Spirit corrects all our seeming problems at their source, healing the ego's content of fear with His love and demonstrating that there is no order of difficulty in miracles or problem-solving.

attack T458f,461; M21

Course M3

death W311

dream T351; W339f

ego T274; M77

fear T230,302,347,569; W402

forgiveness W243,344,**357-59**

God M79

Holy Spirit **T106f,506f**; W105

idol T577,586f

illusions T348,453f,609; M64

problems W139,141

reason **T442f**

sickness W263; M18

special function T495

special relationships ... T319,335f

suffering T545

free will

existent only in the illusory world of perception, where it appears that the Son of God has the power to separate himself from God; since on this level we chose to be separate, we can also choose to change our mind; this freedom of choice — between wrong- and right-mindedness — is the only one possible in this world.

creating T14f,16,70

ego T130

God T55,426

Heaven/hell M51

Holy Spirit T145,184

Jesus T85,**134f**

mind T10,177

peace/guilt T386

time .... T intro.,79,301f; W315,434; M4

world M75

free will — A

an aspect of our free will: we are free to believe what reality is, but since reality was created by God we are not free to change it in any way; our thoughts do not affect reality, but do affect what we believe and experience to be reality.

function

knowledge: creation, the extension of God's love or spirit; God created His Son, Christ, Who in turn creates as does His Father; our function of creating, ongoing throughout eternity, is restored to our awareness when the Atonement is completed.

perception: forgiveness, healing, salvation, the acceptance of the Atonement for ourselves; our "special function" is to forgive our special relationships.

the function of the Holy Spirit is to carry out the plan of the Atonement, giving each Son of God his special function.

Atonement M53

creating T117,123,**138f**,156,214,228,572f

forgiveness T**260**; W103,104,105f,**355f**,456

healing T156,214,228; W255f; M54

holy relationship T349f,448f

Holy Spirit T216,449; W109f,281,391; M67

salvation W107,**174-76**,177f,**342-44**,449

sin T527

special function T**403f**,**493f**,495-97,500,505f,507f, 509; W173

teacher of God W278; M11,15,**18**,35f,37,40

vision W56

gap

the illusory space between ourselves and others, brought about by the belief in separation; in this space arise the dreams of sickness and hate, since projection must always follow a belief in separation.

gift

knowledge: the gifts of God are love, life and freedom, which can never be withdrawn, though they can be denied in this world.

perception: w-m: the ego's gifts are fear, suffering and death, though they often are not seen for what they are; the ego's gifts are "bought" through sacrifice.

      r-m: God's gifts are translated by the Holy Spirit into forgiveness and joy, which are given us as we give them to others.

see: *giving/receiving*

altar	T270; W183
brother	T177,543,571; W448
Christ	W442
ego/God	T55,120; W110
forgiveness	T406,449; **W214f,367f**,437,459
freedom	T135; W369
God	T104,116,181; W**185f**,223,**308-10**, 429,437
grace	W316
gratitude	W216f,367f
healing	M19,21f
Holy Spirit	T257,271,406,449; W427
Jesus	T135,397f; M55
lilies/thorns	**T397-99**
limitless	T518; M68
miracles	W466
real world	T621
special relationships	T472
teacher of God	M12,21
world	W185,277

giving/receiving

w-m: if one gives he has less, reinforcing the ego's belief in scarcity and sacrifice and exemplifying its principle of "giving to get"; believing it can give its gifts of guilt and fear away, the ego's version of giving is really projection.

r-m: giving and receiving are identical, reflecting Heaven's principle of abundance and law of extension: spirit can never lose, since when one gives love one receives it; spirit's gifts are qualitative, not quantitative, and thus are increased as they are shared; the same principle works on the ego level, for as one gives guilt away (projection) one receives it.

see: *gift*

abundance T52,118f
bargain T104,154
creation W**185**
extension/projection ... T120f
forgiveness T**394f**; W211,213,**222-24**,369,465
God T181
healing T256; W256; M19,54
holy relationship T403,445,448,567; M5
Holy Spirit T72,97f,162,402; W436,473
idea T67,72; W**345f**
law of love W394,465,466,468
miracle T1f,163,503; W293f,466
sacrifice T52; W345f
teacher of God W**281-83**; M13,**19f**,21,42
vision T621; W**191f**,292
Word of God W188
world W185

God

the First Person in the Trinity; the Creator, the Source of all being or life; the Father, Whose Fatherhood is established by the existence of His Son, Christ; God's essence is spirit, which is shared with all creation, whose unity is the state of Heaven.

body T97,364,462
Cause/Effect T28,256,**259,550**; W454
Christ T152,**187**,213,292; W421
creation T14,63f,**104f**; W414,**451**
crucifixion T32f
death T217,389; M63f
dependency T190
ego T77f,179; W122f
Father T178; W393
fear T149,303,391f,393,558,563,602
forgiveness T326,471; W73,412
healing T105,109-11
holy instant T294
Holy Spirit T68,**69-71**,78,241,274,299; W427; M85f
Jesus T5,39,621f; M55f
judgment/justice T29f,**498f**; W**445**; M37,47f
last step T105,199,241,532; M65,75
laws T95,174,293; W132f
laws of chaos T174,455-58
loneliness T19,298
love T151,217-19,226f,294,391f; W73,313,34
miracles T1-4
perception/knowledge .. W67
prodigal son T138
relationship T299,333
sacrifice T33,303
salvation W120f

God (cont'd)

grace

an aspect of God's Love in this world; it is our natural state as spirit, awareness of which is returned to us when we complete our lessons of forgiveness; thus it is past learning for it cannot be taught, but is the goal of learning for all lessons point to its love.

Atonement T33

forgiveness T492

healing T374; W255

holy instant W316f

holy relationship T373f,383,445

Holy Spirit W317,427

Jesus T383

Love W313f,315,467

miracle T8,520; W334,463,468

salvation W316,437

Son of God T126,193

spirit T7

teacher of God M69

vision T492; W313

gratitude

the expression of thanks to our Creator for our existence, and to all living things that offer the opportunity for remembering Him; our gratitude to each other reflects our recognition that salvation comes through forgiveness, and thus becomes the way to remember God; God is also grateful to His creation for completing Him, and along with the Holy Spirit and Jesus, He is grateful for our efforts to return to Him.

see: *song of Heaven*

brother (Son of God) .. T**62f**,66,114,201,235f,315,**339f**,430, 486; W196,362f,**367f**

Christ (from) W368; M12

God (from) T177,**486**,522,537; W232,368

God (to) T88,235; W216,**362f**; M**55**,88

Holy Spirit (from) T339,352; M86

Holy Spirit (to) T379; W352,369; M68

Jesus T88,135,621f; M55

Jesus (from) T352; M68f

miracle T3

song T622; W216,435,444; M12

Great Rays

knowledge: the extensions of the Light of God, our true reality as Christ; the Great Rays are of the spirit, having nothing to do with the body at all.

perception: the presence of the light of Christ; seemingly separated from the Great Rays of God which are unseen, this light is manifest as a spark in each Son, made visible through forgiveness of our special relationships.

guilt

the feeling experienced in relation to sin; the total of all the negative feelings and beliefs we have about ourselves, largely unconscious; guilt rests on a sense of inherent unworthiness, seemingly beyond even the forgiving power of God, Whom we believe demands punishment for our sin of separation against Him; guilt will always be projected in the form of attack, either onto others as anger or onto our bodies as sickness.

see: *scarcity principle*

happy dream

the Holy Spirit's correction for the ego's dream of pain and suffering; though still illusory, the happy dream leads beyond all other illusions; it is the dream of forgiveness in which the real world is seen and salvation attained.

having/being

the state of the Kingdom, where there is no distinction between what we have and what we are; an expression of the principle of abundance: all that we have comes from God and can never be lost or lacking, including our Identity as His Son; an integral part of the lessons of the Holy Spirit.

ego/Holy Spirit T56
God T110,133,516
Holy Spirit T99f,102f
Kingdom T56,64,108
life T118
mind/spirit T67
Son of God T182,275

healing

the correction in the mind of the belief in sickness that makes the separation and the body seem real; healing is based on the belief that our true identity is spirit, not the body, thus sickness of any kind must be illusory, as only a body or ego can suffer; healing is the effect of joining with another in forgiveness, shifting perception from separate bodies, the source of all sickness.

Heaven

the world of knowledge, wherein dwell God and His creation in the unity of His Will and spirit; though exclusive of the world of perception, Heaven can be reflected here in the holy relationship and the real world.

Atonement	T74,77,448
body	T97,364,366,505
changelessness	T249,262,282,570
communication	T107
creations/extension	T101,**104f**,106f,117,120,123,242, 313,315,489
decision	T511; W232,233f,**257-59**
ego	T56,**74f**,280f
forgiveness	T509f,516,**591**; W243,359,374,464
grace	W316
gratitude	T395,522
guilt	T77,248,261,263
having/being	T56,94,108
healing	T105f,272
hell	T228,280-83,318,440,459f,491f,496; W248
holy instant	T282f,335
holy relationship	T**349**,357,378,380f,399,402,425,448, **521f**
Holy Spirit	T69,81,91,100,107,131,281f,367, 429; W290
illusions	T172,440,459
inheritance	T44,209,262
Jesus	T104,247,349
joy	T65,113,126,323
justice	T501,509; M47f
light	T91,452,488,521f,585; W177,408, 418,429

Heaven (cont'd)

love	T93,317; W344,359,430
miracle	T241f
peace	T128,249f,272,385,573
real world	T196,271,452,508f,621; W125,293, 408,442
sin	T378,403,441,498,510f
Son of God (Self)	T80,127,178,313,358f,490; W469
special relationships	T291,317f
teacher of God	T127; M36
Thoughts of God	T75,587
truth	T103,107,110,250
unity	T54,270,**359**,518
vision	T378,413,421
will/Will	T124,130,209,270,352,585; W342
within	T**54**,197,304; W135
world	T137f,248f,317

hell

the ego's illusory picture of a world beyond death which would punish us for our sins; hell thus is the guilt of the past projected into the future.

body	W415
decision	T509,619; W232,257f; M12,51,78
dream	W339; M66
ego	T280f; W69
fear	T617; W364
forgiveness	T471; W374,464
guilt	T281; W60; M14
Heaven	T228,496,523; W233f
Holy Spirit	T281; W477; M67
Jesus	M83
sacrifice	W248
sin	T498,515; M2
special relationships	T318,469,471
suffering	M65
teacher of God	M36
unreality	T228,281; W339,464

holy instant

the interval of time in which we choose forgiveness instead of
guilt, the miracle instead of a grievance, the Holy Spirit instead of
the ego; it is an expression of our little willingness to live in the
present, which opens into eternity, rather than holding on to the
past, which keeps us in hell.

holy relationship

the joining in Christ's vision of two people who once perceived each other as separate; the Holy Spirit's means to undo the guilt of an unholy or special relationship by shifting the goal to forgiveness or truth.

body T405; W415

Christ T437f,441,604f

faith T338,343f

forgiveness T393-95,435,448-50,491f

holy instant T337,340

Holy Spirit T337-40,407,447f; M5

Jesus T132,353f,383,385

joining T404f,435f; W339f; M5,6f

light T353f,441,448

real world T337

sin T443f,444f

special function T349f,403f,493f,507

special relationships ... T406-9,435

vision T405f,441

Holy Spirit

the Third Person of the Trinity Who is God's Answer to the separation, and is the communication link between God and His separated Sons; He sees our illusions (perception), leading us through them to the truth (knowledge); the Voice for God Who speaks for Him and for our real Self, reminding us of the Identity we forgot; also referred to as Comforter, Guide, Mediator and Teacher.

Holy Spirit (cont'd)

Teacher	T210f,283f,311,483f; M67f
teacher of God	W220f,**281f**,436; M25,36,69,86
time	T281-83,511
Trinity	T67,72,483
Voice for God	T70; W78,187,271-73,**342-44**; M85f
world	T329,487f; W105

humility/arrogance

humility is of the right mind, which recognizes its dependence on God, while arrogance is of the wrong mind, which feels it is in competition with Him; spirit rests in the grandeur of God, from Whom it derives its power, while the ego's grandiosity comes from believing that *it* is God, with the power to determine our function in God's plan; in this way the ego confuses humility with arrogance, telling us we are unworthy to be God's instruments of salvation.

ego	T50,156
function	W101,281,**342-44**
grandeur/grandiosity	T**165-67**
holy instant	T355
Holy Spirit	T308
Jesus	T286f
littleness/magnitude	T**285-88**,288
love	T178
sin	T375,378,389,501
teacher of God	M36
truth	W450
wish/will	T449,518
world	W236f,**274f**

"I am as God created me"

an expression of the principle of the Atonement: the separation from God never truly occurred; denial of this principle reinforces belief in our separated ego self and body; accepting it heals the separation, restoring to awareness our true Identity as God's Son, our Self.

arrogance T518
Atonement W261f; M55
body W376
Cause/Effect W454
changelessness T587; W274,396,425
Christ T233f; W421,441,471; M85
decision W260
ego M77
forgiveness W356,408,441,468
freedom T513; W93
Great Rays W474
guiltlessness T222,234
holiness W430,438; M66
Holy Spirit M67f
illusions T469f; W422
judgment W405,419; M54
justice T507
light W101,401
love W402,423,428
mind T102
resurrection T193
sacrifice W452,465
salvation W160,**162f,195f,300f**
Self W368,416,431
sin T375
suffering T177,**620f**; W407,428; M18
truth T453; W252,353
unity W164,341,443,451; M30
will W444
world T476; W237f

"ideas leave not their source"

the expression of the law of cause and effect, for cause and effect cannot be separate: a thought cannot leave the mind that thought it.

knowledge: the extension of God, His Son, has never left its Source, for what is of God can never be separate from Him.

perception: w-m: projecting guilt from our mind by attack reinforces its presence in the mind that thought it.

r-m: extending the love of the Holy Spirit through forgiveness — seeing Him in others — increases our awareness of His loving presence in ourselves.

attack T472; W40,318
body T443; W122,395
Christ W294,421
creation T90,517; W291
creations T312
extension T91
giving T67; W345
Holy Spirit T389
idol T576
life/death T388; W311f
love/fear T114
mind T374,433; W71
projection T515,517
salvation W148,168
separation T372,440f
sharing T75,92
sin W287
Thought of God T587,609; W306,414,426,454
world W231,236f,403

idol

symbol of the substitution of the ego for our true Self or God; a form of special relationship, projected onto people, things or ideas; a false belief that there can be something other than, and separate from God; the anti-Christ.

anti-Christ	T575-77
body	T407,409
death	T573-75; W302
decision	T584,586-88
dream	T577f
fear	T113,579; W318-20
holy relationship	T592f
illusions	T588-90; W119
Jesus	M84
real world	T590-92
self-concept	T610; W101,147
sickness	T171-73,594f
special relationships	T586

illusion

something that is believed to be real but is not; the ultimate illusion is the separation from God, upon which rest all the manifestations of the separated world which may properly be called distortions in perception; i.e., seeing attack instead of a call for love, sin instead of error; the illusions of the world reinforce the belief that the body has a value in and of itself, a source of either pleasure or pain; forgiveness is the final illusion as it leads beyond them all to the truth of God.

attack T143,226,**588-90**
death M63f
decision T**509**,609
defense T445-47; W**245f**,266,278; M39
ego W21; M77
fear T**188**,318
forgiveness T**325f**,470f,568; W73,243,369f
form/content T63,230
holy instant T325f
Holy Spirit T115,137
mind T115,118,556; W71f,110; M75
miracle W152
resurrection M65
sacrifice W452
sin T327,515,541
special relationships ... T**314-16,318-20**,344
truth T103,327f,438f,**453f**,558; W**189f**,284f

innocence

knowledge: used rarely to denote God or His attributes.

perception: w-m: the face of innocence the ego employs to conceal its true intent of attack, by making others guilty for having inflicted suffering upon an innocent victim.

r-m: the Holy Spirit's correction for our belief in sinfulness; awareness of our innocence as God's Son is restored to us through the forgiveness of our guilt and attainment of true perception.

invulnerability

our natural state as a Son of God; our true nature being spirit and not the body, nothing of the ego's world can harm us; recognizing our invulnerability becomes the basis for our defenselessness, the condition for forgiveness.

Atonement T256f

attack T84f,92,**209f**,461,489; W**40**,115,150

defenselessness W**277f**; M13

forgiveness W**103**,210,213

gentleness M11f

God T175,217,461,479; W**75f**,79,150,361, 405,416,456

guiltlessness T222f,**256**; W172

holy instant T604f

Holy Spirit T88,92; W424; M39

innocence T390,451

Jesus T84-87,137

love T171; W415

real world W433

sickness T144

sinlessness W**461**,464

spirit T9,51,615

unity/wholeness T54,75; W451

Jesus

first person or "I" of the Course; the one who first completed his part in the Atonement, enabling him to be in charge of the whole plan; transcending his ego, Jesus has become identified with Christ and can now serve as our model for learning and an ever-present help when we call upon him.

(Note — not to be exclusively identified with Christ, the Second Person of the Trinity.)

Atonement T**6f**,62,**76**; M85

awe T5,13

Christ T10; M**83f**

Christmas T286,301f,305f

comforter W478

Course M56

crucifixion T**84-87**

decision T39,70f,**134f**

Easter T396f

ego T50f,59,136f

elder brother T**5**,57

fear T25,216

forgiveness T385,396,397f; M84

God T**139**,288,**621f**; M**55**

gratitude T62f,88,352; M55

holy instant T302

holy relationship T333,353,385f,394f

Holy Spirit T71,75,240,395; M85f

illusions W119

light T133f

miracle T6-8,23

model T71,84-87; M55f,83f

resurrection T39,47,193,217,264; W**322**; M83f

sacrifice T302,305f

Second Coming T58

Jesus (cont'd)

judgment

knowledge: strictly speaking God does not judge; the Course's references to God's Judgment reflect His recognition of His Son *as* His Son, forever loved and one with Him.

perception: w-m: condemnation, whereby people are separated into those to be hated and those to be "loved," a judgment always based on the past.

           r-m: vision, whereby people are seen either as expressing love or calling for it, a judgment always based on the present.

see: *Last Judgment*

attack	T220,581f; W467
body	T410f; W271f
dream	T577-80
ego	T58,80,144f,273f
fear	T596
forgiveness	W369-71,391,470
God	T29f; W445; M28,37,47f
Holy Spirit	T101,155f,200-2,216,273-75; W220, 272f,446,467; M25,66
love	T499f; W225
past	T290
perception	T41-44,216; W81,446; M23
special relationships	T466
teacher of God	M11,26f
vision	T405,413,415; W468

justice

the Holy Spirit's correction for the world's injustice; the belief that God's Sons are equally loved and equally holy, undoing the judgments based on separation; justice is the end of sacrifice and is called the rock on which salvation rests.

attack T522-24

forgiveness T509

God T505,507,512; M47f

Holy Spirit T497-501,501f

judgment T578

mercy T43

miracle T502f,506f

sin T498-501

Kingdom of God, Heaven

(see: Heaven)

knowledge

Heaven, or the pre-separation world of God and His unified creation in which there are no differences or forms, and thus it is exclusive of the world of perception; not to be confused with the more common use of "knowledge," which implies a subject who "knows" and an object which is "known"; here it reflects pure experience with no subject-object dichotomy.

(Note — since perception and knowledge are usually discussed together, *perception* is not cross-referenced below.)

Christ T213; W291f

Course T369; W257

creation T37,45; W291

ego T37,51

faith T373

forgiveness W**369**,371,460; M15,79,82

grace W313,315-17

Holy Spirit T68,**90**,170,213; W67,427; M85

Jesus T39

mind T38

miracle T40f,310

peace T128

real world T195,195f,238; W229

reason T427

resurrection T39

revelation T36

spirit T38f,47f

true perception T**35-37**,54,61,68,219,241; W25; M**81f**

truth T515; W409

wholeness T41,144,240

world W403

Last (Final) Judgment

equated with the end of the Atonement when, following the Second Coming, the final distinction is made between truth and illusion, all guilt is undone, and awareness is restored to us of our Identity as God's beloved Son.

fear T29f; M37
Holy Spirit M66
miracle T30
perception/knowledge T41; W445
Second Coming W439
truth/illusion T508f

last step

this step, belonging to God, occurs when the Atonement is complete and all ego interferences are removed; when nothing remains to separate us from God He takes the last step, raising us unto Himself; strictly speaking God does not take steps, and the term actually refers to our return to the Father we never truly left.

Atonement T300

face of Christ M79

forgiveness T260,532,**591**; W99,**359**

grace W313,315

Holy Spirit T102,**105**,379; W388

Jesus T62

memory of God T550

miracle T242,554

real world **T199**; W229,432,433; M75

resurrection M65

true perception T241; M82

laws of God

the principles that express God's existence and the extension of His Kingdom.

knowledge: the actual laws include creation, love and truth.

perception: reflected in this world these laws become forgiveness, healing and freedom, in contrast with the ego's laws of projection and death, the laws of chaos.

body W292,425

Christ W471

creation T114,169,489

death T476; W255

decision W239-41

ego T78,243

extension/projection ... T106f,120f

forgiveness T493; W369

freedom T174; W93f,151

giving T118; W293,463,468

healing T109f,476,529,537

holy instant T293

holy relationship T403f,406

Holy Spirit T106f,120; W281

inviolate T133,151

laws of chaos T174,458

love T236,487; W225f,465

miracle T539; W135,466

perception T487,489

protection T168,186,589

truth T515

world T126,220; W132f; M8,45

lilies

symbol of forgiveness, the innocence of God's Son; the gift of forgiveness that we offer each other, contrasted with the ego's gift of thorns.

altar T412; W346

face of Christ T396

innocence T399

Jesus T397f

light W457

miracle W463

truth W460

love

knowledge: the expression of God's relationship to His creation, which is unchanging and eternal; it is beyond definition and teaching, and can only be experienced or known.

perception: love is expressed through forgiveness; it is the emotion given us by God, in contrast to the ego's emotion of fear, and is manifest by any expression of joining with another.

Atonement T16,26,325
attack T114,209-11,458f,461-63,522; W114f; M21
body T12,359,**364-66,406f**,564
Christ T187,203f,**213**,592
Course .... T intro.,228
creating T104f,113f,138,169
death T390; M63f
ego T115,207f,290
extension T104,120,181,222,464,550
faith T373,421
fear T12,66,190,**202,225-27,230-33**,302,347, 382,391f,**563f**; W182,318f
forgiveness T369,492,568; W**73**,344,358f
God T119,151,176f,**217-219**,226f,294f,299, 321; W174-76,**225f**
grace W313,315
gratitude T201; W362f,437
guilt T220f,**246f**,297,382
happy dream T238,570
healing T147,537
holy instant T**290-92**,293f,305,366
Holy Spirit T163f,200,258,264,273-75,300; W427,436
identity T87,92,111,115; W112,321,396,428,469
invulnerability T171,217; W**79**,415,417,467
Jesus T104f,247f,305f; M55
judgment T411; W470

magic

the attempt to solve a problem where it is not, the ego's strategy to keep the real problem — the belief in separation — from God's Answer; guilt is projected outside of our minds onto others (attack) or our bodies (sickness) and sought to be resolved there, rather than undone in our mind by the Holy Spirit.

attack M**42-44**,45

ego T29,53

guilt M43f

healing T111f,160

Holy Spirit M59

sickness T**19f**,21,78,173; W263f

temptation M39-41

world W79,132f

make/create

spirit creates, while the ego makes.

knowledge: creation occurs only within the world of knowledge, creating truth.

perception: making leads only to illusions; also referred to as miscreating.

ego/Holy Spirit T78
ego/spirit T49f
fear/love T28,114
forgiveness T369
healing T23f
mind T29,38,77
projection/extension ... T179
Self W160
separation T37,39f
teacher of God M12,18
thought T1,44; W26
wish/will W125
world T195

means/end

despite the multitude of means in the world, there remain but two ends or goals: truth or illusion; the body can serve either end, as the mind elects.

w-m: the body is used as a vehicle for sin and guilt, reinforcing illusion through the special relationship.

r-m: the body is used for forgiveness, leading us to truth through the holy relationship.

body T**143-46**,362,386,405; W409,**415**,435

forgiveness W145,**412**

God T479f; W413

grace W313

holy relationship T340,357

Holy Spirit T**409-11,422**; W427,440

perception T**479-81**,483

reason T429,440

salvation W449

truth T**340-42**,346

vision W420

world T608; W38

memory of God

the final stage of the Atonement, which follows seeing the face of Christ, and precedes the last step, taken by God Himself; we remember God through forgiveness and healing, undoing all beliefs in separation that obscured His Presence to us.

body T453
Christ's vision W422
decision T218; W339
face of Christ T510,521,592; W213; M79
fear T225,391,549f; W77
forgiveness T369f; W99,397,427,460,468
function W451,475
grace W313
gratitude W448
guilt T223,225,246
healing **T203**
holy instant T294,549
innocence T602
Jesus M83
last step T550; W**433**
resurrection M65
sacrifice T504f,507
special function T508
true perception M82

mind

knowledge: the activating agent of spirit, to which it is roughly equivalent, supplying its creative energy.

perception: the agent of choice; we are free to believe that our mind can be separated or split off from the Mind of God (wrong-mindedness), or that it can be returned to it (right-mindedness); mind does not refer to the brain, which is a physical organ and thus an aspect of our ego or bodily self.

attack T114,359f
body T19f,21f,359f,371; W167,245-47,355
creation T20,21,27
death W311f
decision T114,134f,207; M16f
denial T118
ego T60,115f,208
extension T91f,117,142f
guilt T77f; W118
healing T160,553
Jesus T39,134f
joining T359f,553; W29
law of mind T90f,106,215
make/create T38,44f
mind-training T13; W1
miracle T549,553
sickness T142; W247; M16f
sin T423,606f
spirit T10,38; W167,170,456; M75
world T206f; W236-38,351f

Mind of God

knowledge: the aspect of God through which His spirit creates His Thought; as extensions of God, the Minds of Christ and the Holy Spirit share in the attributes of the Mind of God; One-mindedness.

perception: after the separation the Mind of Christ appeared to be split in two: Mind and mind.

changelessness T168,201,320,357
Christ T68; M75
creation T58,120,**180f**,495
guiltlessness T222
healing T371
Holy Spirit T**68**,72,91,241,262; W174,316
identity T163,166f,240; W261
innocence T262
Jesus T**71**,75f,113
light T354,485f; W418
love T177; W217
miracle T549
sinlessness W55
thoughts W67,**71f**,98,168,266f
Thoughts T90,185,476; W92,426,454
Trinity T35
unity T113,136,175,587f; W58
will T69,471

miracle

the change of mind that shifts our perception from the ego's world of sin, guilt and fear, to the Holy Spirit's of forgiveness; it is the expression of joining with another that corrects and undoes the error of separation; miracles transcend the laws of this world to reflect the laws of God; they are performed by the Holy Spirit through us, being the means of healing ourselves and others.

Atonement T17,19f
body T12
correction T9; W463
decision T256; W137f
dream/happy dream ... T551-53,568f; M78
ego M77f
extension T123,309
forgiveness T539; W463; M78
God W135f,152
healing T19,472,529,535,553-55,594f,598
holy instant T535; W316
Holy Spirit T69,158,214,272-76,310; W273
Jesus T6-8,10
justice T502f
principles T1-4,23f
revelation T4f
salvation W153
sin T538f
time T6,10,30; W170
vision T36; W154-56,293f

Name of God

the Identity of God, Which Self we share as His Son; the symbol of God's holiness, which is our own as well.

Christ T201,286; M54

creations T178,184f

forgiveness W402

Holy Spirit T81,212,295,379; W138,316

illusions T316

love W428

Jesus T147,333; M55

salvation W187,397

Son of God T147; W334f,379,393,416,431,472; M18,87

Teacher of teachers M61

unity T518; W261,337f

"no order of difficulty in miracles"

the first principle of miracles; something is either true or false, with no real levels existing within each category; there is no order of difficulty in correcting illusions as they are all equally unreal, requiring only the miracle's shift from illusion to truth; similarly, there is no order of difficulty in healing as any form of sickness (illusion), even unto death, is undone when brought to truth.

One-mindedness

the Mind of God or Christ; the extension of God which is the unified Mind of the Sonship; transcending both right- and wrong-mindedness, One-mindedness exists only at the level of knowledge.

Christ M75,85
Holy Spirit T53,68

perception

level I: the post-separation world of form and differences, mutually exclusive of the world of knowledge; this world arises from our belief in separation and has no true reality outside of this thought.

level II: perception comes from projection: what we see inwardly determines what we see outside of ourselves; crucial to perception, therefore, is our interpretation of "reality," rather than what seems to be objectively real.

w-m: perception of sin and guilt reinforces the belief in the reality of the separation.

r-m: perception of opportunities to forgive serves to undo the belief in the reality of the separation.

see: *true perception*

(Note — since perception and knowledge are usually discussed together, *knowledge* is not cross-referenced below.)

body T38

change T35-37,399f,515

consciousness T**37**; M75f

decision T191f,214f,425,**483,487-89**; W**231f**

dream T238,351

forgiveness W369,427,**460**; M79

God W**67**,357

Holy Spirit T68,90,213,241,422; W67,403; M85

interpretation T35,38,40

judgment T41,41f; W446; M**23**

law T90,487,612; W349

learning M8

mind T38,425,427

miracle T35f; W463,466

part/whole T144,240f

prayer T41

projection T231,**415**,480; W81,441

perception (cont'd)

periods of unsettling

our guilt and fear cannot be undone without dealing with them through the opportunities for forgiveness given us by the Holy Spirit; this is what leads to the periods of discomfort and anxiety we almost inevitably feel in the process of shifting from wrong- to right-mindedness.

prayer

belongs to the world of perception, as prayer is asking God for something we believe we need; our only real prayer is for forgiveness, as this restores to our awareness that we already have what we need; as used here, prayer does not include the experiences of communion with God that come during periods of quietness or meditation.

Bible T152

forgiveness T40

Holy Spirit T152-55; M68

joining W417

justice M48

miracle T1,40

Name of God W335,389

perception T41

words M51f

projection

the fundamental law of mind: projection makes perception —
what we see inwardly determines what we see outside of
ourselves.

w-m: reinforces guilt by placing it onto someone else,
      attacking it there and denying its presence in
      ourselves; an attempt to shift responsibility for
      separation from ourselves to others.

r-m: the principle of extension, undoing guilt by extending
      (projecting) the forgiveness of the Holy Spirit.

attack T**84f**,89,231; W33,40,**318f**,364f
authority problem T43
body T359f,387
cause/effect T552; W28,49
crucifixion T87f
dream T**539-43,543-46**
ego T89-91,119,120f; W**120**
extension/law of mind . T14,90,106,120,179,215
fear T77,351; W21,231,298
forgiveness T491f; W391
God W114,122
guilt T220,**223f**,244,**244f**; W118; M43
perception T231,**415**; W4,13,231,**454**
sacrifice T32f,498,523
separation T**88f**
sin T606,610f
special relationships ... T314f,317-20,330f,443f
world T243,**347f**,413f,540,**545**; W18,19,53,
                       236f

questions

the Course presents our basic decision to choose between God and the ego in the form of different questions.

real world

the state of mind in which, through forgiveness, the world of perception is released from the projections of guilt we had placed upon it; thus, it is the mind that has changed, not the world, and we see through the vision of Christ, which blesses rather than condemns; the Holy Spirit's happy dream which is the end of the Atonement, undoing our thoughts of separation which allows God to take the last step.

bridge T322,513

consciousness M76

death M64

decision T**508f**; W229f

face of Christ M79f

forgiveness T**328-30,368-70**,452,**590-92**,593f; W408,432,**433**

God T28,207,219

happy dream T238,579; W397

holy relationship T337,592

Holy Spirit T195,212f,330,421,495

Jesus T216

judgment T400f; W446

last step T199; W433

light T368; W130f,**349**

perception/knowledge .. T194f,195f,369

sickness T197

sin T433; W330

vision T212f,236-38; W293f,432

reason

right-mindedness; thinking in accordance with the Holy Spirit, choosing to follow His guidance and learn His lessons of forgiveness, seeing sinlessness or error rather than sin, choosing vision instead of judgment.

(Note — not to be confused with rationalism.)

defenselessness T445

ego T424,442

forgiveness T528

guilt T246f

holy instant T429f,434

holy relationship T443f

Holy Spirit T424,426f,429; M21

madness **T428f**

perception/knowledge .. T427

real world T329

separation T426

sin/error T428,442f

truth/falsity **T439f**

world T436

resurrection

the awakening from the dream of death; the change in mind that overcomes the world and transcends the ego, allowing us to identify completely with our true Self; also refers to the resurrection of Jesus.

(Note — since crucifixion and resurrection are usually discussed together, *crucifixion* is not cross-referenced below.)

revelation

the direct communication from God to His Son which reflects the original form of communication present in our creation; it proceeds from God to His Son, but is not reciprocal; brief return to this state is possible in this world.

right-mindedness

the part of our separated mind that listens to the Holy Spirit — the Voice of forgiveness and reason — and chooses to follow His guidance rather than the ego's, and thus return to One-mindedness.

sacrifice

a central belief in the ego's thought system: someone must lose if another is to gain; the principle of giving up in order to receive (giving to get); e.g., in order to receive God's love we must pay a price, usually in the form of suffering to expiate our guilt (sin); the reversal of the principle of salvation or justice: no one loses and everyone gains.

Atonement	T**32-34**
attack	T302,504
body	T384,422f,**504f**,566f,574,607
Christ	T304
ego	T124f; W450
fear	T33,564; W453
giving	T52; W185,**345f**; M19
God	T32f,108,302-4,496f,607; W341,452, 465
guilt	T302,305
Holy Spirit	T422f,501f,506; W133
Jesus	T304-6
judgment	T596f
justice/injustice	T**497f**,500f,**502f**523
laws of chaos	T456f
love	T302-4,**304-6**
miracle	W135
real world	T495
salvation	T460,**496f**,517
special relationships	T296f,**318f**
suffering	T525; W179,346
teacher of God	W284-86; M8-10,**32-34**
truth	W157
vision	W42,56,355f

salvation

the Atonement, or undoing of the separation; we are "saved" from our belief in the reality of sin and guilt through the change of mind that forgiveness and the miracle bring.

cause/effect T**545f**,552

compromise T460

face of Christ M79

forgiveness T590; W73,103,**174-76**,213f,344,437; M35

function W174-76,177f,316,342-44,449

God T288; W120f

guilt T257f; W**118f**

happy dream T329f,590; W**397**

healing W254

holiness T443; W56,60

holy relationship T63,132,385

Holy Spirit T258; W168,316,369

illusions T320; W119

justice T503; M47

mind T206; W**236f**,275

miracle T598; W170

perception T509; W67

real world T195,330,508f

reason T442

right-mindedness T53

rock of salvation T**496f**

sacrifice T519; W465

simplicity T304,600; W153

sin W179

teacher of God M3,6

thoughts W23,26,34

vision T411,614

world T493,586,614

scarcity principle

an aspect of guilt; the belief that we are empty and incomplete, lacking what we need; this leads to our seeking idols or special relationships to fill the scarcity we experience within ourselves; often associated with feelings of deprivation, wherein we believe others are depriving us of the peace which in reality *we* have taken from ourselves; contrasted with God's principle of abundance.

attack T119

body T**305,573f**

decision T57

ego T**52**,206

God T561; W307

Holy Spirit T76

love T293

need M35

perception T4,40f

projection T14,24

separation T**11**,39

sin T78

special relationships/idols ... T319,435,574f,586

truth/error T9

Second Coming

the return to awareness of our reality as the one Son of God, which we had at our creation, the First Coming; it precedes the Last Judgment, after which this world of illusion ends.

awareness of reality ... T159f

ego T58

forgiveness W**439**

Jesus T**58**

Last Judgment T158; W439

Self

our true Identity as Son of God; synonymous with Christ, the Second Person of the Trinity; contrasted with the ego self we made as a substitute for the Self That God created; used rarely to refer to the Self of God.

attack	T465; W114,329
body	W415
Christ/Son	T73,**292**,620; W158,162,166,170,196, 411,**421**,441
ego/self	T52,365f,613; W160,**167f**
fear	W295f
forgiveness	T474f
God	T292; W**411**,334
healing	W254-56
Holy Spirit	W168,210,477
illusions	T12,558
Jesus	W322
love	W112f,321,410,415
miracle	T426
salvation	T186; W236f
sinlessness	W330
unity	W**164-66**,346
world	W225,227,410

"senseless musings"

trying to understand ideas that are beyond our comprehension; most often used for the world of knowledge, but occasionally refers to the ego as well.

ego T51,117; M73

God/Heaven T185,261,480,591; M56

identity W261,469

knowledge T369

oneness T508; W316

salvation T590,614f; M35,61f

Teacher of teachers M61

separation

the belief in sin that affirms an identity separate from our Creator; the separation seemed to happen once, and the world which arose from that thought is symbolized by the ego; it is a world of perception and form, of pain, suffering and death; the separation is real in time, but unknown in eternity.

Atonement T16,18,90,331

attack T226,449f

body T359,**371f**,561,563f,614

decision T320

dissociation T88

ego T55,77,190f; W457

fear T50; W231

guilt **T220,290**

Holy Spirit T68,331f,334

magic M43

mind/thought T45,241,440; W87

origin **T14f**,45,552

perception T37f,41; W336

projection **T88f**,552

salvation W177,397

sickness T514,**553f**; W254; M54

sin T428f

world T207; W237f

sickness

a conflict in the mind (guilt) displaced onto the body; the ego's attempt to defend itself against truth (spirit) by focusing attention on the body; a sick body is the effect of the sick or split mind that caused it, representing the ego's desire to make others guilty by sacrificing oneself, projecting responsibility for the attack onto them.

see: *suffering*

Atonement	W263; M53f
attack	T144f,560
body	T**144-46**,566f; W251-53
cause/effect	T551,553-55
decision	W**250-53**; M16-18,53
God	T**171-73**,173-75,182,558
guilt	T**525-27**; W263; M17
healing	T372,557; W118,254-56,263f
love	T203
magic	M20,78
mind	T19f,**146-48**,553; M**16-18**
miracle	T2,552f,594f
separation	T142,182,**553f**,555-57,557f; W**254**; M54
sin	T514f; W472

sin

the belief in the reality of our separation from God, which separation is seen by the ego as an act incapable of correction; this belief in sin leads to guilt, which demands punishment; sin is equivalent to separation, and is the central concept in the ego's thought system, from which all others logically follow; to the Holy Spirit, sins are errors to be corrected and healed.

Atonement	T362f
attack	T490f
body	T409,410f,538f,**606f**
death	T375,383,388f,494,498; W179
defenses	T82,399,446
error	T**374-76,376-78**,428f,**442f**,501; M45
fear	T15,**423f**,451,520; W414
forgiveness	T488f; W210,**242-44**,391; M83
guilt	T78,376f; M43,81
illusion	T327,515; W**179f**,242,**409**; M81
projection	T517,606,610f
punishment	T374f,376f,455f
sacrifice	T422f,497f,500
separation	T428f,586
sickness	T514f,525-27; W472
special relationships	T421f,435,443f,**467**,470,472f,474
suffering	T539
world	T413f,494-96; W330; M35

Son of God

knowledge: the Second Person of the Trinity; the Christ Who is our true Self.

perception: our identity as separated Sons, or the Son of God as ego with a wrong- and right-mind; the phrase "son of man" is used rarely to denote the Son as separated.

Cause/Effect T420,550

Christi/Self T**187,620**; W159f,162,195f,**421**,471; M30,75

creation T14,88,560; W266,**451**

crucifixion T193f

forgiveness T595; W138

God T10,182,269,298f,406; W**445**

grace T126

guiltlessness T221-23,225,261,601f; M3

Heaven T505

holy relationship T349,404,408

Identity W**353f**,410,**469**

immortality T182,572

Jesus T5,76

light W101

Name T147; W138,316

son of man T225,481,482; M30

Trinity T35

unity T75,136,198; W164,261

song of Heaven

symbol of the love and gratitude that unites God and His Sons, who once believed they were separate from their Creator.

ancient T**416f**; W298
Christ T475; W304
Easter T398
freedom T248,339,425,505
gratitude T235,**510**,622; M12
holy relationship T337,511
Holy Spirit W369f
love T467,505,511,602
praise T248,446
resurrection M66
salvation T621
special relationships ... T467
time T512,579; M87

special relationships

relationships onto which we project guilt, substituting them for love and our relationship with God; as all special relationships retain guilt, they reinforce belief in the scarcity principle, doing what they would defend; all relationships in this world begin as special since they begin with the perception of separation, which must then be corrected by the Holy Spirit through forgiveness, making the relationship holy; there are two forms of special relationships: special hate justifies the projection of guilt by attack; special love conceals the attack within the illusion of love, where we believe our special needs are met by special people with special attributes, for which we love them; in this sense special love is roughly equivalent to dependency.

attack T**294-97,313-16**,472f,473-75

body T321,330f,406-9,472,476-78

death T335f,474

ego T307,**333-36**

fear T315,466

forgiveness T468,**470f**,488,492-94

God T10,294,317,471

guilt T245,247,290f,292,295-97,314,
317-20,321-23

healing T529

holy instant T**290-92**

holy relationship T337-40

Holy Spirit T291,298,323,334,483,493

past T323f,**330-33**

sacrifice T296,318f

scarcity T435,573-75,**586**

separation T290,563

sin T435,443f,**466-70**,470,472f

substitution T291,347f,**464-66**

spirit

the nature of our true reality which, being of God, is changeless and eternal; it is contrasted with the body, the embodiment of the ego, which changes and dies; spirit's energy is activated by the mind, to which it is roughly equivalent.

body	T22,392,**614f**; W167
communication	T9,63
creating	T10,38,54,67,**122f**
ego	T**47-51**,53,62
God	T41; M75
grace	T7
Holy Spirit	T73,122
immortality	T54
mind	T9,10,**38**; W**167f**,439,456; M75
miracle	T1-3
Self	W167f,**170f**
soul	M75

star

symbol of Christ, of the light and Presence of God that always shines in us, and which forgiveness reveals.

suffering

one of the basic ego witnesses to the reality of the body and the non-existence of spirit, since only a body can suffer physical or psychological pain; to be in pain, therefore, is to deny God, while being aware of our true invulnerability as God's Son is to deny the reality of pain.

see: *sickness*

attack T542,560,613

body T220,359; W132

decision W351f; M16f

forgiveness W357f,370

God T177,184,228; W351f

guilt T243,376,387

Holy Spirit T125,307,545f

illusions T61f,439

judgment M27

pleasure/pain T384,386f

projection T525f,539-42

sacrifice W346

sin W179

special relationships ... T296,317

teacher of God

at the instant we decide to join with another, a decision to join the Atonement, we become teachers of God; teaching the Holy Spirit's lesson of forgiveness, we learn it for ourselves, recognizing that our Teacher is the Holy Spirit Who teaches through us by our example of forgiveness and peace; also referred to as "miracle worker," "messenger," and "minister of God."

Atonement T22; M53f

body W289f,373; M30f

characteristics M8-15

Christ W309f,471

Course M38f,67

death W303; M63f

defenselessness W278-80

giving W281-83; M21

gratitude W216f,363

healing W255f; M18,19f,21f,53f

Holy Spirit W419,436; M38f,51f,67-69

Jesus T62,65; W322; M84,86

judgment M25,26f,37

light T354; W104,144,218,347f,406; M3

magic M39-41,42-44

miracle T21-24; W468

pupils M4f,6f

reincarnation M57f

salvation W172f,177f,345,469

Teacher of teachers M61,84

Word of God W220,424

world W284-86; M1f,35f,61

teaching/learning

what we believe we are is what we teach, and what we teach reinforces our belief; thus teaching and learning occur all the time, are equal, and cannot be separated from each other; our choice of what we teach and learn is limited to our identity as spirit or ego.

Atonement	T**262-64**,275; M6
attack	T92; M42
body	T145f,566f,606f
change/contrast	T249,252f,615f
decision	W257
ego	T48f,91f,108,311f
equality	T47,98,162; W436; M**1**
forgiveness	W**210f**,357-59; M15
God	T95,259; W357-59
grace	W315
guilt/guiltlessness	T255-59,262-64,601; M3
happy learner	T252-54,262
holy relationship	M4f
Holy Spirit	T95-103,107,109f,129f,141,**210f**,221, 278f,280,311,536f,611f; W210f
Jesus	T48-51,75f,**85-88**,264; W322
levels	M**6f**
love	T intro.,87,92
mind	T48,98f,111
peace	T100,263f,**275-79**
projection	T106
Self	T312f
transfer	T210,536f; W1f
truth	T251f,252-54,275f
vision/knowledge	W289f,291f
world	T**600-3**; W336f

temptation

seeing ourselves and others as egos or bodies, denying our true Identity and wishing to make illusions real.

attack T87,462,606; W121,160,299,361,488; M21

body T619; W105

decision T602,**619-21**

God T326,497; W389

guilt T523,599

illusions T**598f**; W101,105,422

Jesus T87,622

littleness/glory T451f

psychic powers M59f

salvation W118

self T**618f**; W171

teacher of God M**39f**,55

world T476; W133,139,227f

thorns

symbol of crucifixion, the guilt of God's Son; the gift of the ego which projects guilt onto others and attacks them for it; contrasted with lilies, the gift of forgiveness.

body T397-99; W298
crucifixion T396,525
Holy Spirit T506f

Thoughts of God

knowledge: the extension of God's Mind or spirit; includes all of creation, our true Self as well as our own creations; being part of God, His Thoughts share in His attributes: unified, eternal and changeless.

perception: used infrequently to refer to Thoughts of the real world; e.g., peace, salvation, healing, miracle.

changeless T**587f**; W312
Christ/Self W368,421
creation T**90**,104; W190,237,272,**451**,454
ego T59f,365
eternal life T388,587f; W311f
giving/receiving W191f
healing T105
Holy Spirit T241; W344
limitless W426
miracle T41
peace W**397**; M28f,79
real world T322; W418
salvation W174f,461
Self W368
spirit T41; M**75**
truth W252,370,428
unity T90,**609**; W92,155f,**306f**,414
vision W289
world T494

time

level I: an integral part of the ego's illusory world of separation, in contrast to eternity, which exists only in Heaven.

level II: w-m: the means of maintaining the ego by preserving the sins of the past through guilt, projected by fear of punishment into the future and overlooking the present, which is the only time there is.

r-m: the means of undoing the ego by forgiving the past through the holy instant, the time interval of miracles; when forgiveness is complete, the world of time has fulfilled its purpose and will disappear into eternity.

symbol of the world of sin, reflecting its inherent meaninglessness and harmlessness, despite its seeming solidity and strength.

dream T578f

fear T464,590; W278f

guilt W279

idols T578,589f

sin W409

time W466

war W333

world T368; W413; M32

Trinity

consists of God, the Father and Creator; His Son, Christ, our true Self; and the Holy Spirit, the Voice for God; included in the Second Person of the Trinity are our creations; the unity of Its Levels is not understandable in this world.

true perception

seeing through the eyes of Christ, the vision which corrects the misperceptions of the ego; not to be equated with physical sight, it is the attitude that undoes the projections of guilt, allowing us to look upon the real world in place of the world of sin, fear, suffering and death.

see: *perception*

forgiveness T329; W447; M81f
gratitude W232
holy relationship T385f,438
Holy Spirit T249,495; W67,357,420; M85
innocence T34
knowledge T35-37,54,68,213,240f; M81f
light W25
miracle T241
real world T219; W330
right-mindedness T53
world W345

truth/falsity (illusions)

something is either true or false, reality or illusion; there can be
no compromise: we are either created by God or made by the ego;
this principle is the basis for healing and explains why there is no
order of difficulty in miracles, since all that is needed for healing
or the miracle is to shift from illusion to truth.

vision

the perception of Christ or the Holy Spirit that sees beyond the body to the spirit that is our true Identity; the vision of forgiveness and sinlessness through which is seen the real world; vision is purely internal, reflecting a decision to accept reality rather than judge it; thus, it is not to be equated with physical sight.

body	T476; W292
decision	T614; W31,42,43,422
extension	W45,46,55
faith	T421-23
forgiveness	W131,292,294,355f,420
God	W65
Holy Spirit	T212f,398,412-14; W272,403; M85
innocence	T618f; W346,417
Jesus	M56,83
judgment	T405,419; W81
justice	M48
light	T232f,241; W25,191,313
miracle	T36; W154-56,293f
projection	W13,16
real world	T212,621; M75
reason	T442
sinlessness	T410f,411-14,441,467f; W447

Voice for God
(see: Holy Spirit)

war

symbol of the ego's belief in conflict between itself and God; this
conflict is projected into experiencing ourselves at war with the
world and with God.

death	....	M63
ego	....	T108,**430f**
God	....	T452-55
illusions	....	T248,453-55
miracle	....	T462f,535
peace	....	T70,565; M49
Self	....	T558
sin	....	T451
special relationships	...	T464-66,487
Thought of God	......	T588
truth	....	T603; W252

Will of God

the expression of God's being, which can only create; though seeming to be split by the separation, the Will of God's wholeness and unity with the will of the Sonship remains unchanged and unbroken.

changelessness T133,494; M3

Christ T237,246; W291,368; M75

creation T63f,150,174; W389,451; M75

ego/self T110,355,419,452; W159,457

extension/creations T123,**131f**,138f,181f; W133,357,450,**456**

fear T**149f**,182

forgiveness T516; W357,391,458; M79

happiness/joy T12,131,182; W177f,179f,181,400

holy relationship T438,593

Holy Spirit T70f,130,149,353,483f,601

Identity T119,125,**130f**,136

immortality T182,194,209; W302f

Jesus T**134f,136f**,139,287,621

magic W132; M40,43

miracle T125,136

peace T133,174,250,464; M50

real world T352; W88,125

resurrection T193

salvation T138,163

sickness/suffering T173f,176,184f,237f,497; W175f,455

sin T378,512f,**515f**,594f; W409

sinlessness W330,459

special relationships ... T466,467,470f,477

unity T34f,136,148,150f,182,270,380,426f, **486f**; W**128f**,221,342,406,444,454; M18

vision W65,97,131

wish/will T189,590; W91f,443; M79

world W308

wish/will

the ego wishes, the spirit wills.

knowledge: willing expresses creation or truth.

perception: wishing can reflect wrong- or right-mindedness, both inherently illusory, since wishing implies there is a state other than where one is, and there can be no reality outside of Heaven.

death/life T518

decision T124f

dream T590

forgiveness M79

free will T44

learning T601

make/create T473

mind T38,517

truth T515; W91f

world W125f

Word of God

God's answer to the separation; used variously for different aspects of this answer: e.g., forgiveness, peace, Atonement, the Holy Spirit.

(Note — does not refer to Jesus or Christ.)

Atonement M53
attack M33,45
body M31
creation W300,**424**
faithfulness M14
forgiveness W355,460,463
function W203
Holy Spirit W187f,216,**220f**,473,**477**; M85
last step W388
Jesus M55
resurrection M65
Second Coming W439
sinlessness W464
teacher of God W220,406,469; M18,34,35,52
thoughts/words W19f,23,348,397
world M28

world

level I: the effect of the ego's belief in separation, which is its cause; the thought of separation given form; the world, being the expression of the belief in time and space, was not created by God, Who transcends time and space entirely; unless specifically referring to the world of knowledge, *world* refers only to perception, the post-separation world of the ego.

level II: w-m: the world of separation reinforces the ego's belief in sin and guilt, perpetuating the seeming existence of this world.

r-m: the world becomes a place where we learn our lessons of forgiveness, a teaching device the Holy Spirit uses to help us transcend the world; thus the purpose of the world is to teach us that there is no world.

see: *real world*

attack	W**34f**,125,277
body	T543f,614f; M16f,81
death	T220,572f; M63f
dream	T350-52,**539-43**,551-53
fear	T592; W21,245,403
forgiveness	T488,585f; W105; M**35f**
God	T137f,194,609; W23,274f,308; M28,81
guilt	T**220**,243f,367f,526,601
healing	T19,476; W237
Holy Spirit	T74,495f; W403; M59
illusion	T**367f**; W85,284,308,336f,402,**403**
judgment	T400f; M25,26
love	T226; W225f
mind	W**236-38**
projection	T347f,**413f**,415,539-42,544-46; W18,21
sacrifice	T504f; M32

wrong-mindedness

the part of our separated mind that listens to the voice of sin, guilt, fear and attack, and chooses to follow its dictates, imprisoning us still further in the world of separation; almost always equated with the ego.

III. SCRIPTURAL INDEX
(King James Version)

ABBREVIATIONS FOR SCRIPTURAL REFERENCES

OLD TESTAMENT

Gn	Genesis
Ex	Exodus
Lv	Leviticus
Nb	Numbers
Dt	Deuteronomy
Jg	Judges
1 K	1 Kings
Jb	Job
Ps	Psalms
Pr	Proverbs
Qo	Ecclesiastes
Is	Isaiah
Jr	Jeremiah
Ezk	Ezekiel
Dn	Daniel
Ho	Hosea
Jl	Joel

NEW TESTAMENT

Mt	Matthew
Mk	Mark
Lk	Luke
Jn	John
Ac	Acts
Rm	Romans
1 Co	1 Corinthians
2 Co	2 Corinthians
Ga	Galatians
Ep	Ephesians
Ph	Philippians
Col	Colossians
1 Th	1 Thessalonians
1 Tm	1 Timothy
2 Tm	2 Timothy
Heb	Hebrews
1 P	1 Peter
1 Jn	1 John
Rv	Revelation

A: A Course in Miracles
1. Text
2. Workbook
3. Manual

Text

Page	Lines		Quote	Bible Reference
2	3T		Miracles bear witness to truth.	Jn 18:37b
2	11,12T		...it is as blessed to give as to receive.	Ac 20:35
2	17T		It is a way of loving your neighbor as your-self.	Lv 19:18
2		10B	Miracles enable you to ... raise the dead ...	Mt 10:1,8a
5	21T;	9B	... elder brother ... (Jesus)	Rm 8:29
5		15B	"No man cometh unto the Father but by me."	Jn 14:6
5		8-6B	My devotion ... charge of the Sonship ... share it.	Jn 17:22
5		5B	"I and my Father are one."	Jn 10:30
5		4B	... the Father is greater.	Jn 14:28c
6		18,17B	... you do it to *yourself* and me.	Mt 25:40
6		2B	"Heaven and earth shall pass away"	Mt 24:35
6-7		1B to 1T	... the resurrection and the life ...	Jn 11:25
7	3,4T		This is how a man ... what he is.	Pr 23:7
7	18T		"Lead us not into temptation"	Mt 6:13a
7		3,2B	The Golden Rule asks ... do unto you.	Mt 7:12
8	12,13T		When you bring in the stranger ... your brother.	Mt 25:35
9	20T		"There is no death"	Rv 21:4b
9	21,22T		I came to fulfill the law ...	Mt 5:17

Page	Lines		Quote	Bible Reference
9		12B	Those who witness for me . . .	Ac 1:8
10	13T		"Except ye become as little children"	Mt 18:3
10	23T		"God is not mocked" . . . but a reassurance.	Ga 6:7a
10		12B	. . . it cannot serve two masters.	Mt 6:24
10		3B	. . . choosing to follow Him (Christ).	Mt 4:19
10		3B	All shallow roots must be uprooted . . .	Lk 8:13
11	1T		. . . on which the reverse of the Golden Rule rests.	Mt 7:12
11	12T		. . . the "separation," which is the meaning of the "fall" . . .	Gn 3:1-7
12	7T		*Perfect love casts out fear.*	1 Jn 4:18
12	15T		. . . this faith *is* His gift.	Ep 2:8
12		15B	All real pleasure comes from doing God's Will.	Ps 40:8
12		1B	. . . who know not what they do.	Lk 23:34
14	5T		. . . likeness to your Creator . . .	Gn 1:26-27
14-15		6B to 14T	The Garden of Eden	Gn Chapters 2,3
14		2B	. . . disappear in the twinkling of an eye . . .	1 Co 15:52a
15	1T		Yet the Bible . . . a deep sleep fell upon Adam . . .	Gn 2:21
15	19-21T		The knowledge . . . that you *are* free.	Jn 8:32

Text (cont'd)

Page	Lines	Quote	Bible Reference
15	4B	I have asked you to perform miracles . . .	Mt 10:1,8a
15	2,1B	. . . cannot be performed in . . . fear.	Mt 17:19,20
16	2T	. . . where your heart is . . . your treasure also.	Mt 6:21
16	5,6T	. . . "the peace of God which passeth understanding."	Ph 4:7
16	3B	. . . the only defense . . . not a two-edged sword.	Rv 1:16
17	13,12B	"The meek shall inherit the earth."	Mt 5:5
18	2T	Perceiving the body as a temple . . .	1 Co 6:19
19	15T	. . . daily bread.	Mt 6:11
23	14T et passim	charity	1 Co 13:13
24	16,17T	"Father forgive them . . . what they do."	Lk 23:34
24	20T	"Be of one mind"	2 Co 13:11
24	21T	"Do this in remembrance of me"	Lk 22:19
24	7,6B	*I do not have to worry . . . will direct me.*	Mt 10:19
27	9,10T	. . . thought and belief . . . move mountains.	Mt 17:20a
28	15B	Whenever light . . . the darkness is abolished.	1 Jn 1:5
28-29	2,1B to 1T	"For God so loved the world . . . everlasting life."	Jn 3:16
29-30	Title et passim	. . . Last Judgment	Mt 11:22
30	16,15B	. . . God Himself looked . . . it was good.	Gn 1:31
32	6B	"Vengeance is Mine, sayeth the Lord"	Rm 12:19

Text (cont'd)

Page	Lines	Quote	Bible Reference
33	3,4T	. . . that God rejected Adam . . . Garden of Eden.	Gn 3:23-24
33	10,11T	. . . my injunction . . . Father in Heaven is merciful.	Lk 6:36
33	15,16T 15,14B	"lamb of God . . . sins of the world"	Jn 1:29
33	19T	The lion and the lamb . . . together . . .	Is 11:6
33	21T	"Blessed are the pure . . . see God"	Mt 5:8
33	2B	. . . light abolishes forms of darkness.	1 Jn 1:5
34	6,7T	. . . Atonement, not sacrifice . . .	Ho 6:6
34	4,3B	. . . your own mind . . . likeness of His Own . . .	Gn 1:26,27
35	4,5T	. . . commends his Spirit . . . Hands of his Father.	Lk 23:46
35	11T	. . . their hearts are pure . . .	Mt 5:8
35	15,16T	"When He shall appear . . . see Him as He is."	1 Jn 3:2
36	19B	The Bible tells you to know yourself . . .	Mt. 7:3-5; 23:25,26
37	2T	"Alpha and Omega, the beginning and the end"	Rv 21:6
37	3T	"Before Abraham was I am."	Jn 8:58
37	4T	"Fear God and keep His commandments"	Qo 12:13
39	17T	"Many are called but few are chosen"	Mt 20:16b
39	20T	. . . find rest unto their souls.	Mt 11:29b

Text (cont'd)

Page	Lines	Quote	Bible Reference
40	15B	. . . the truth that shall set you free . . .	Jn 8:32
40	2B	"God created man . . . image and likeness"	Gn 1:26-27
41	1B	"Judge not that ye be not judged"	Mt 7:1
44	20,21T	"Seek ye first the Kingdom of Heaven"	Mt 6:33
44-45	2B to 3T	The "devil" . . . direct opposition to God.	Mt 4:1-11; Rv 12:7-10
45	4T	. . . "sell" him their souls . . .	Mt 16:26
45	9,10T	The fruit . . . in the symbolic garden.	Gn 2:16-17
46	6T	There is no death . . .	Rv 21:4b
46	7T	The branch that bears no fruit . . .	Jn 15:2
46	5B	Your kingdom is not of this world . . .	Jn 18:36
47	1,2T	The Bible says . . . twice as far as he asks.	Mt 5:41
47	11,12T	"Be still and know that I am God."	Ps 46:10
49	5,4B	. . . be still and know that God is real . . .	Ps 46:10
49	4B	. . . and you are His beloved Son . . . well pleased.	Mt 3:17
49	1B	God is not the author of fear.	1 Co 14:33
50	20,21T	Do not try to make . . . house stand.	Mt 7:24-27
50	21T	Its weakness is your strength.	2 Co 12:9b
50	16B	Of your ego you can do nothing . . .	Jn 5:19,30

Page	Lines		Quote	Bible Reference
50		12B	The meek shall inherit the earth . . .	Mt 5:5
51	3,4T		I could not understand . . . tempted . . . myself.	Mt 4:1-11; Heb 2:18
51	9-11T		*In this world . . . I have overcome the world.*	Jn 16:33
52		20B	Be patient a while . . .	Ps 46:10
54		18,17B	"The Kingdom of Heaven is within you"	Lk 17:21
54		5B	*. . . the ego will not prevail against it.*	Mt 16:18b
55		10,9B	The Bible gives . . . gifts . . . must ask.	Mt 7:7a,8a
55-56		1B to 1T	Thou shalt have no other gods before Him . . .	Ex 20:3
56	4T et passim		. . . Holy One . . .	Ps 16:10
57	7T		The glass in which the ego . . . is dark indeed.	1 Co 13:12
57	16T		. . . darkened glass.	1 Co 13:12
58		14B	To the ego's dark glass . . .	1 Co 13:12
58		13,12B	. . . the Holy One shine on you in peace . . .	Nb 6:25,26; Ps 16:10
59	12,13T		You and your brother . . . in my name . . .	Mt 18:20
59	13,14T		I raised the dead . . .	Jn 11:43-44
59		18B	All things work together for good.	Rm 8:28
60		15B	"Seek and ye shall find."	Mt 7:7b,8b
62		12,5B	. . . Holy One . . .	Ps 16:10
64		12B	The Bible . . . you should praise God.	Ps 111:1; 150:1-6; Rm 15:11
66		7B	. . . to love his neighbor except as himself.	Lv 19:18

Page	Lines		Quote	*Bible* Reference
67		14,13B	"May the mind . . . also in Christ Jesus."	Ph 2:5
67		9B	. . . the Comforter . . .	Jn 14:16a
67		7,6B	"If I go . . . He will abide with you."	Jn 14:16b; 16:7
70	13,14T		God did not leave His children comfortless . . .	Jn 14:18
70		18,17B	What profiteth it . . . lose his own soul?	Mt 16:26
70		10B	. . . God's Will is done . . . as it is in Heaven.	Mt 6:10b,c
71	1,2T		. . . all power in Heaven and earth.	Mt 28:18
71	11T		You are the light of the world with me.	Mt 5:14; Jn 8:12
71		12,11B	"My yoke is easy and my burden light."	Mt 11:30
74	15T		. . . but truth can still set you free.	Jn 8:32
74	17T		. . . in remembrance of me.	Lk 22:19
74		5,4B	The ego cannot prevail against the Kingdom . . .	Mt 16:18b
75	6,7T		. . . your own thoughts can make you . . . free.	Jn 8:32
75		19B	and of such is the Kingdom of Heaven.	Mt 19:14
75		7,6B	"turning the other cheek."	Mt 5:39
76	15T		. . . rendering unto God . . . that are God's?	Mt 22:21
76		9B	You can indeed depart in peace . . .	Lk 2:29
76		8B	. . . because I have loved you as I loved myself.	Lv 19:18; Jn 13:34
80	3,4T		The Mind that was in me *is* in you . . .	Ph 2:5
80		19B	"As ye sow . . . ye reap"	Ga 6:7b

Page	Lines		Quote	Bible Reference
80		16B	"Vengeance is mine, sayeth the Lord"	Rm 12:19
80		11,10B	"I will visit the sins . . . and fourth generation."	Ex 34:7
80		5B	"The wicked shall perish"	Ps 37:20
81	8,9T		. . . bearing false witness to God Himself.	Ex 20:16
81	14,15T		"thine is the Kingdom"	Mt 6:13b
81	16T		"I am come as a light into the world"	Jn 12:46
82	4,5T		. . . cast your cares . . . He careth for you.	1 P 5:7
82	10,11T		They have not moved mountains by their faith . . .	Mt 17:20a
82	12,13T		. . . healed the sick . . . not raised the dead.	Mt 10:1,8a
82		21,20B	God commended His Spirit . . . yours to Him.	Lk 23:46
84-88		13B (84) to 8B (88)	crucifixion (of Jesus)	Mt 27:26-50
86	12T		My brothers slept . . . the "agony in the garden" . . .	Lk 22:39-46
86	17T		. . . on them that I must build my church.	Mt 16:18a
86		8,7B	. . . the way, the truth and the life.	Jn 14:6
87		19,18B	. . . out of . . . the "wrath of God" . . . weapon . . .	Lk 21:23; Jn 3:36
87		12B	"I come not to bring peace but a sword."	Mt 10:34
87		9,8B	"Betrayest thou the Son of Man with a kiss?"	Lk 22:48
87		7,6B	The "punishment" . . . upon Judas . . . a similar mistake.	Mt 26:24

Page	Lines	Quote	Bible Reference
87,88	2B to 1T	As you read . . . the Apostles . . . at the time.	Jn 16:12
88	9B	. . . you will have learned of me . . .	Mt 11:29a
90	11T	. . . everything was created by Him and in Him.	Jn 1:3
90	14B	. . . He uses everything for good . . .	Rm 8:28
90	7B	The ego cannot prevail against this . . .	Mt 16:18b
91	16,15B	The ego is legion . . .	Mk 5:9
91	12,11B	. . . light of the world.	Mt 5:14; Jn 8:12
92	11B	. . . the truth that will set you free . . .	Jn 8:32
97	17T	To be of one mind is meaningful . . .	1 P 3:8
105	10T	. . . that your joy may be complete . . .	Jn 15:11
105	13B	. . . true in the beginning . . . and . . . true forever.	Heb 13:8
107	1B	"I am with you always"	Mt 28:20
108	2T	. . . *you* are the way, the truth and the life.	Jn 14:6
110	8B	Seek ye first the Kingdom of Heaven . . .	Mt 6:33
110	5B	God is All in all . . .	1 Co 15:28
110	4,3B	All being is in Him . . . your being is His.	Ac 17:28
113	12,11B	. . . your remembrance of me . . .	Lk 22:19
113	4B	Blessed are you . . .	Mt 5:3-11
113	2B	Come therefore unto me . . .	Mt 11:28a

Text (cont'd)

Page	Lines	Quote	Bible Reference
119	4T	. . . Sons of the living God . . .	Jn 6:69
119	8,9T	. . . they are His beloved Sons . . . well pleased.	Mt 3:17
122	9B	. . . spirit's own fullness . . .	Ep 3:19
122	8,7B	The ego cannot prevail against . . .	Mt 16:18b
125	10,9B	. . . Who has not left you comfortless.	Jn 14:18
126	7T	Following Him . . .	Mt 4:19
127	18,19T	"What is truth?"	Jn 18:38
131	5T et passim	. . . power and glory . . .	Mt 6:13b
131	22B	Glory to God in the highest . . .	Lk 2:14
131	21B	Ask and it shall be given you . . .	Mt 7:7a,8a
132	15T	For I am . . . with you . . .	Mt 28:20
132	15,16T	. . . in remembrance of *you.*	Lk 22:19
132	15,14B	He will be imprisoned . . . decision . . .	Mt 16:19b
133	13B	Yet He is All in all.	1 Co 15:28
133	8B	I am come as a light into a world . . .	Jn 12:46
133	5B	I said that I am . . . end of the world . . .	Mt 28:20
133	1B	. . . to overcome the world.	Jn 16:33
134	5T	The remembrance of me . . .	Lk 22:19
134	6T	. . . of Him Who sent me to you . . .	Jn 8:16
134	13,14T	The world therefore must . . . reject me . . .	Jn 15:18
135	18T	Of yourself you can do nothing . . .	Jn 5:19,30

Page	Lines		Quote	Bible Reference
135	20-23T		I will always remember you . . . of God.	Lk 22:19
138	9,10T		. . . over His Kingdom the world has no power.	Jn 18:36
138	14-21T		Listen to the story . . . prodigal son . . . nothing else.	Lk 15:11-32
139		10,9B	Whom God has joined cannot be separated . . .	Mt 19:6
140	2,3T		Your heart lies where your treasure is . . .	Mt 6:21
141	19T		Rejoice, then, that . . . you can do nothing.	Jn 5:19,30
141		17B	"The word (or thought) was made flesh."	Jn 1:14
142	7T		. . . temple of the Holy Spirit . . .	1 Co 6:19
142		21B	. . . working through the body, but not *in* it.	Jn 15:19
143	9,10T		. . . thought cannot be made flesh.	Jn 1:14
146		7,6B	All forms of sickness, even unto death . . .	Jn 11:4
147		14B	The Bible enjoins you to be perfect . . .	Mt 5:48
147		14B	. . . to heal all errors . . .	Mt 10:1,8a
147		14,13B	. . . to take no thought of the body as separate . . .	1 Co 6:15-20
147		13,12B	. . . to accomplish all things in my name.	Jn 14:13,14
150	10T		It is impossible . . . in alien tongues.	Gn 11:1-9; 1 Co 12:10,28
151	7T		God is Love . . .	1 Jn 4:8,16
152		2B	The Bible . . . all prayer is answered . . .	Mt 21:22

Page	Lines	Quote	Bible Reference
153	21B	This light can shine into yours . . .	Mt 5:16
154	9-7B	What you give . . . exact measure . . . upon it.	Mt 7:2
157	14T	. . . is not *of* you but *for* you.	Jn 15:19
160	19B	"Let there be light"	Gn 1:3
161	13B	*"By their fruits ye shall know them . . ."*	Mt 7:16
162	3T	What you offer . . . you offer to Him . . .	Mt 25:40
162	13,14T	If what you do to my brother . . . to me . . .	Mt 25:40
169	3,4T	. . . you love your creations as yourself . . .	Lv 19:18
169	9T	. . . your banishment is not of God . . .	Gn 3:23-24
171	13T	What Comforter can there be . . .	Jn 14:16a
172	17,18T	"My peace I give unto you"	Jn 14:27
172	18-14B	. . . it is . . . makes you whole . . . faith in me.	Mt 9:22
172	10,9B	But have no other gods before Him . . .	Ex 20:3
172	9,8B	God is not jealous . . . you make . . .	Ex 20:5
173	7,8,21T 5B	. . . other gods before Him.	Ex 20:3
174	13,14T	If you perceive other gods . . .	Ex 20:3
174	19,18B	. . . there are no other laws beside His.	Ex 20:3
175	3B	. . . the wages of sin *is* death.	Rm 6:23

Page	Lines	Quote	Bible Reference
176	17,16B	Yet the Son . . . Who alone is his Help.	Ps 115:9
176	15B	. . . of yourself you can do nothing . . .	Jn 5:19,30
180	17,18T	There are no beginnings . . . in God . . .	Heb 7:3
180	20T	I and my Father are one with you . . .	Jn 10:30; 14:20
182	15B	Blessed are you . . .	Mt 5:3-11
183	18,19T	. . . know not what you do.	Lk 23:34
183	15,14B	. . . your guest will abide with you.	Jn 14:16b
184	19T	. . . the Comforter of God is in you.	Jn 14:16a
184	19,18B	Your Comforter will rest you . . .	Mt 11:28b, 29b
184	10,9B	. . . for he knows not what he does . . .	Lk 23:34
184	4,3B	. . . your joy would be complete!	Jn 15:11
185	16B	The children of light . . . in darkness . . .	1 Th 5:5
185	13,12B	. . . there *are* no other gods . . . before Him . . .	Ex 20:3
185	10B	Only God's Comforter can comfort you.	Jn 14:16a
187	19B	But love yourself . . . Love of Christ . . .	Jn 13:34 Ep 3:19
187	17B	Come unto me . . .	Mt 11:28a
187	7B	Blessed is the Son of God . . .	Ps 118:26
187	2B	Peace be unto you . . .	Jn 20:19, 21a, 26
188	12T	Be not afraid . . .	Jn 6:20

Page	Lines		Quote	Bible Reference
192	5T		. . . false witness . . .	Ex 20:16
192	13,14T		"Blessed are ye . . . and still believe."	Jn 20:29
192	17,18T		. . . ascends to the Father . . .	Jn 20:17
193	1T		I am *your* resurrection and *your* life.	Jn 11:25
193	9,10T		For we ascend unto the Father together . . .	Jn 20:17
193	10,11T		. . . as it was . . . ever shall be . . .	Heb 13:8
193		11B	The Father has given . . . that is His . . .	Lk 15:31
193		7,6B	. . . the nails . . . last thorn from his fore-head.	Mt 27:29,35
194	2,3T		You have nailed . . . crown of thorns . . . head.	Mt 27:29,35
194	20T		. . . your Redeemer liveth . . .	Jb 19:25
194		10,9B	To God all things are possible.	Mt 19:26
194		5,4B	The Bible speaks of . . . a new earth . . .	Is 65:17
196	9T		The Bible tells you . . . as little children.	Mt 18:3
196		10B	. . . you will see it as it is . . .	1 Jn 3:2
196		4B	. . . if you ask you will receive.	Mt 7:7a,8a
197	18,19T		Blessed are you . . .	Mt 5:3-11
197		21,20B	The Kingdom of Heaven *is* within you.	Lk 17:21
198	15,16T		If you perceive offense . . . from your mind . . .	Mt 5:29
203		15B	. . . know your brother as yourself.	Lv 19:18

Page	Lines		Quote	Bible Reference
204	16T		A little while and you will see me . . .	Jn 16:16
204		19B	There is no fear in perfect love.	1 Jn 4:18
204		9B	The Lord is with you . . .	Lk 1:28
204		8B	Yet your Redeemer liveth . . .	Jb 19:25
204		8B	. . . abideth in you . . .	Jn 14:16b
205	13,14T		I once asked . . . sell . . . and follow me.	Mt 19:21
208	6T		. . . "Seek and do *not* find."	Mt 7:7b,8b
209	9,10T		If death is your treasure . . . purchase it.	Mt 13:44-46
209	12,13T		Your inheritance . . . bought nor sold.	Gn 25:31-33
211-12		1B to 1T	. . . gain the . . . world . . . your own soul.	Mk 8:36
215	5T		. . . for what you seek you will find.	Mt 7:7b,8b
220		9,8B	Adam's "sin" . . . out of paradise.	Gn 3:23-24
222	14,15T		Goodness and mercy . . . followed him . . .	Ps 23:6
225	16,17T		. . . great joy in Heaven . . . homecoming . . .	Lk 15:7
227		6,5B	. . . departing in peace . . .	Lk 2:29
227		5B	. . . returning to the Father?	Jn 14:12,28E
228	17T		. . . the dust out of which . . . you were made.	Gn 2:7
232	9T		You who know not what you do . . .	Lk 23:34
232		6,5B	And He . . . return unto the Father . . .	Jn 14:12,28E
233	11,12T		. . . they have risen in Him to the Father.	Col 2:12

Page	Lines		Quote	Bible Reference
234	5,21T	20B	. . . born again . . .	Jn 3:3,7
235		14B	. . . the light is in you.	Mt 5:14
238	10T		The peace of God . . . your understanding . . .	Ph 4:7
238		14B	Your Father knoweth . . . need of nothing . . .	Mt 6:8,32
240	11T		My peace I give you.	Jn 14:27
242		6B	. . . the gates of Heaven . . .	Gn 28:17
243	17,18T		For faith is . . . treasured . . . to you.	Mt 6:21
244	14T		. . . great is the joy in Heaven . . .	Lk 15:7
245		2B	. . . born again.	Jn 3:3,7
247	4T		There is no fear in love . . .	1 Jn 4:18
247	18,19T		No one who condemns . . . peace of God.	1 Jn 2:9
247		11B	I thank You, Father . . .	Mt 11:25
247		9B	. . . my faith . . . on what I treasure.	Mt 6:21
248	10T		. . . the gates of Heaven . . .	Gn 28:17
249		3,2B	They will not prevail against . . .	Mt 16:18b
249-50		1B to 1T	If that suffices Him . . . for you.	2 Co 12:9a
250	18,19T		His certainty suffices.	2 Co 12:9a
251	1T		Yes, you are blessed indeed.	Mt 5:3-11
253	4,5T		Have faith in nothing . . . you seek.	Mt 6:21
253		4B	. . . the light . . . into the darkness . . .	Jn 1:5
253		3B	. . . lets it shine on you.	Nb 6:25
254	19,20T		. . . and built on truth.	Mt 7:24-27

Page	Lines		Quote	Bible Reference
256	13T		. . . replace darkness . . . with love.	1 Jn 1:5; 4:18
256	13-15T		If he . . . binds himself . . . light with him.	Mt 16:19b
258	5,6T		. . . the innocence that sets you free.	Jn 8:32
259	11T		*"He leadeth me and knows the way . . ."*	Ps 23:2,3
262		16B	You know not what you do . . .	Lk 23:34
263		6B	Peace, then, be unto everyone . . .	Jn 20:19, 21a, 26
264	2T		Abide with me . . .	Jn 14:16b
264	4T		Blessed are you . . .	Mt 5:3-11
264	7T		. . . holy ground.	Ex 3:5
264		11B	Judge not . . .	Mt 7:1
266	14T		You know not what you say . . .	Lk 23:34
268		2,1B	All honor to you through Him . . .	1 Tm 6:16; Rv 5:12-13
274		17B	. . . two or more join together . . .	Mt 18:20
275		6B	. . . His Son, given all power by Him . . .	Mt 28:18
277	13,14T		God's Son . . . no needs . . . will not meet.	Mt 6:8,32
283	8T		. . . ascend unto your Father.	Jn 20:17
283		3B	Blessed is God's Teacher.	Mt 5:3-11
284	3,4T		For you are . . . and will forever be.	Heb 13:8
284	8,9T		. . . uphold its (ego) weakness . . . strength.	2 Co 12:9b
284		4-1B	God's Teacher . . . your strength . . . in you.	2 Co 12:9b

Text (cont'd)

Page	Lines		Quote	Bible Reference
286		19,18B	The power and the glory . . .	Mt 6:13b
286		15B	All honor of God.	Rv 5:12-13
287	1,2T		. . . the Prince of Peace . . .	Is 9:6
287	16T		Welcome me not into a manger . . .	Lk 2:7
287	17T		My Kingdom is not of this world . . .	Jn 18:36
287	18T		. . . because it is in you.	Lk 17:21
287	20T		. . . abide with you.	Jn 14:16b
287		9-7B	. . . that we may release . . . would be bound . . .	Mt 16:19b
291	3T		And love . . . is not perfect.	1 Jn 4:18
293	2T		. . . perfect love is in you.	Lk 17:21; 1 Jn 4:18
293	2,3T		And so you seek . . . cannot find without.	Mt 7:7b,8b
293		3,2B	For the instant . . . he is not bound.	Mt 16:19b
305		8B	The Prince of Peace . . .	Is 9:6
310	20,21T		. . . glad tidings . . .	Lk 1:19
311	5T		. . . joyful tidings . . .	Lk 1:19
311		4B	"By their fruits ye shall know them . . ."	Mt 7:16
313	17,18T		His Kingdom has no limits and no end . . .	Dn 7:27
313		9B	Your bridge is builded stronger . . .	Mt 7:24-27
315	9,10T		. . . seek and find all of the barriers . . .	Mt 7:7b,8b
318		20B	"Seek but do not find?"	Mt 7:7b,8b
320	9T		. . . raise other gods before Him . . .	Ex 20:2-3
325		14,13B	Release your brothers . . . perceive in them.	Mt 16:19b

171

Text (cont'd)

Page	Lines		Quote	Bible Reference
325		4B	His help suffices . . .	2 Co 12:9a
326	1T		Seek and *find* His message . . .	Mt 7:7b,8b
326		9-1B	*"Forgive us . . . You love. Amen."*	Mt 6:9-13
327	1T		The betrayal of the Son of God . . .	Lk 22:48
327	16T		You cannot be faithful to two masters . . .	Mt 6:24
332	17T		Whom God has joined . . . put asunder.	Mt 19:6
336		2B	Let us ascend . . . to the Father . . .	Jn 20:17
337	1T		. . . the power and the glory . . .	Mt 6:13b
339	1,2T		. . . justification for your faith . . .	Rm 3:28
339		19,18B	. . . will leave you comfortless . . .	Jn 14:18
341		3B	. . . deception cannot prevail against you.	Mt 16:18
348		19B	. . . "God is not fear, but love" . . .	1 Jn 4:8,16; 4:18
348		4B	. . . the living God . . .	Jn 6:69
349	9T		. . . holy ground . . .	Ex 3:5
352		2,1B	The light is . . . . Darkness . . . put it out.	Jn 1:5
357		9B	"Thy Will be done"	Mt 6:10b
357		2B	. . . love your brother as yourself.	Lv 19:18
365-6		1B to 1T	The desert becomes a garden . . .	Is 51:3
366	9T		. . . living water . . .	Jn 4:10
373	13T		. . . faith is always justified.	Rm 3:28
373		20B	Faith is the gift of God . . .	Ep 2:8

172

Page	Lines	Quote	Bible Reference
374	14T	. . . glad tidings . . .	Lk 1:19
375	16T	For the wages of sin *is* death . . .	Rm 6:23
378	4B	. . . look upon your brother as yourself.	Lv 19:18
378	3,2B	. . . weary ones can come and rest.	Mt 11:28b, 29b
382	18,17B	Perception cannot obey two masters . . .	Mt 6:24
383	10,9B	. . . table of communion. And I will . . . still.	Mt 26:29; Lk 22:30
385	21B	. . . I . . . overcame the world . . .	Jn 16:33
388	6-9T	For what is sent . . . returning it to you.	Mt 7:7b,8b
390	7B	. . . babe of Bethlehem . . .	Lk 2:12
390	5B	. . . the resurrection and the life.	Jn 11:25
394	9,10T	He has . . . forgive your sin . . . for him.	Mt 16:19b
395	5T	He leadeth you and me . . .	Ps 23:2-3
395	11T	. . . garden of seeming agony and death.	Lk 22:39-46
395	13T	. . . rise again . . .	Mt 20:19
395	15,16T	. . . not to be lost but found . . .	Lk 15:24,32
396	14,13B	Let him not . . . the temptation . . .	Mt 6:13a
396	4B	I was a stranger and you took me in . . .	Mt 25:35
397	4B	. . . is against me still . . .	Mt 12:30
398	5,4B	There *is* no fear in love.	1 Jn 4:18
398	3B	Let us lift up our eyes together . . .	Ps 121:1

Page	Lines		Quote	Bible Reference
402	6,7T		. . . this day enter with him to Paradise . . .	Lk 23:43
402	18,19T		. . . faith . . . is justified.	Rm 3:28
402	19T		There is no fear in perfect love . . .	1 Jn 4:18
402		18,17B	. . . the pure in heart see God . . .	Mt 5:8
402		17,16B	. . . Son to lead them to the Father.	Jn 14:6
404	1T		The ark of peace . . . two by two . . .	Gn 7:9
404		14,13B	. . . making straight your path . . .	Is 40:3
406		16B	What is he . . .	Ps 8:4
406-8	Title et passim		The Temple of the Holy Spirit	1 Co 6:19
407	2-6T		Love wishes . . . known . . . misunderstood.	1 Co 13:4-7
408	8T		You are an idolater no longer.	Ep 2:19
408		13,12B	. . . look you not back . . .	Gn 19:26
408		1B	. . . Everlasting Arms.	Dt 33:27
415	4,5T		As a man thinketh . . . perceive.	Pr 23:7
421	20T		. . . faith can move mountains?	Mt 17:20a
422		4,3B	. . . its recognition is at hand.	Mt 3:2
425		13B	The still, small Voice . . .	1 K 19:12
429	7-10T		If you choose sin . . . of safe return.	Mt 16:19b
430	6,7T		To give is . . . to receive.	Ac 20:35
430	18T		God is not mocked . . .	Ga 6:7a
430		9,8B	And you are for him or against him . . .	Lk 9:50
431	4T		. . . they do not know . . . whom they hate.	Lk 23:34

Page	Lines	Quote	Bible Reference
431	21,20B	Yes, it can . . . *seek* . . . never find . . .	Mt 7:7b,8b
431	10B	. . . seek no longer . . . there to find.	Mt 7:7b,8b
435	1,2T	. . . whom God hath joined have come together . . .	Mt 19:6
437	5B	For no two brothers can unite . . .	Mt 18:20
442	6,5B	. . . the rock on which its church is built . . .	Mt 16:18a
446	13,14T	. . . what can separate whom He has joined . . .	Mt 19:6
447	16T	. . . he will seek for it . . . can be found.	Mt 7:7b,8b
451	18T	. . . fear no evil.	Ps 23:4
451	3B	. . . lead God's Son into temptation.	Mt 6:13a
454	7B	. . . the house of God . . . itself divided.	Mt 12:25
454	6B	. . . Holy One . . .	Ps 16:10
454	6,5B	. . . temple . . . becomes a house of sin.	Jr 7:11
457	16T	. . . this priceless pearl . . .	Mt 13:46
463	10T	. . . have a mind as one.	Ph 2:2
464	4T	He will not fail.	Dt 31:6,8
468	12-14T	He has not lost the power to forgive . . . for you.	Mt 16:19b
468	19T	. . . the key to Heaven . . .	Mt 16:19a
469	11T	You *are* your brother's . . .	Gn 4:9
469	10B	. . . the gates of hell . . .	Mt 16:18b
469	7B	The key you threw away . . .	Mt 16:19a

Text (cont'd)

Page	Lines	Quote	Bible Reference
470	19,20T	. . . given your brother's birthright . . .	Gn 25:31-33
470	11-9B	What rests on nothing . . . every breeze.	Mt 7:24-27
471	1T	. . . a flaming sword . . .	Gn 3:24
471	10T	"Thy will be done"	Mt 6:10b
471	20T	. . . Holy One . . .	Ps 16:10
471	18,17B	. . . come forth and waken . . . dream of death.	Jn 11:11
471	14B	Curse God and die . . .	Jb 2:9
471	6,2B	. . . the print of nails . . .	Jn 20:25
472	9-7B	. . . your treasure house barren . . . destroy.	Mt 6:19
473	12T	So are you bound . . . are one.	Mt 16:19b
474	11T	. . . hated him before it hated you.	Jn 15:18
476	22-17B	Look on your brother . . . release you both . . .	Mt 16:19b
476	15,14B	. . . everything that lives and shares His Being.	Ac 17:28
478	8B	This is your son, beloved of you . . .	Mt 3:17
480	2,1B	". . . my own beloved son . . . well pleased."	Mt 3:17
481	7B	The son of man . . .	Ezk 2:1 et passim; Mt 8:20
482	14T	The son of man . . .	Ezk 2:1 et passim; Mt 8:20
482	1B	. . . everlasting Love.	Jr 31:3
483	7,8T	And you must see your brother as yourself.	Lv 19:18
489	8,7B	. . . that his joy might be increased . . .	Jn 15:11

Page	Lines		Quote	Bible Reference
490	20T		In you is all of Heaven.	Lk 17:21
491		20B	. . . returning unto God what is His Own.	Mt 22:21
494	10T		. . . the cost of sin is death.	Rm 6:23
495	2T		For God and His beloved Son . . .	Mt 3:17
497	4,5T		This is the rock on which salvation rests . . .	Mt 16:18a
497		7B	. . . one divided still against himself . . .	Mt 12:25
497		5B	. . . only little faith is asked of you.	Mt 17:20a
498	21T		Vengeance is alien to God's Mind . . .	Rm 12:19
498		9-7B	Nor . . . lightning bolts . . . angry Hand.	Ps 144:67
499	6T		. . . Heaven's gate?	Gn 28:17
499		13B	. . . mercy stand at God's right hand . . .	Ps 110:1
499		13,12B	. . . Son of God . . . to forgive . . . sin.	Mt 9:6
500		16B	Judge not . . .	Mt 7:1
501	16T		. . . you know not what it is.	Lk 23:34
501		18,17B	. . . Heaven . . . the treasures . . . kept for him . . .	Mt 6:20
504		8,7B	For you must see him . . . see yourself.	Lv 19:18
505		9B	He is the same forever.	Heb 13:8
505		9B	Born again . . .	Jn 3:3,7
508-13		14B to 6B	. . . the gate of Heaven.	Gn 28:17
510	12T		The holy place on which you stand . . .	Ex 3:5

Text (cont'd)

Page	Lines	Quote	Bible Reference
511	1,2T	And how great . . . the joy in Heaven . . .	Lk 15:7
512	4,3B	Let the dead . . . be peacefully forgotten.	Mt 8:22
514	14T	. . . in Whom all power . . . rests.	Mt 28:18
514	13B	. . . gifts that are not of this world . . .	Jn 14:27; 18:36
515	15T	It is in this world . . . a part of it.	Jn 15:19
517-18	1B to 1T	What God calls . . . be forever one . . .	Mt 19:6
520	14,15T	You have been told that everything . . . from God.	Rm 8:28
520	7,6B	What profits freedom in a prisoner's form?	Mt 16:26
521	21,20B	The ground . . . is holy ground . . .	Ex 3:5
521	10,9B	And now you stand on ground so holy . . .	Ex 3:5
522	14B	. . . temple of the living God . . .	1 Co 6:19
523	18,17B	. . . you do not know him *as* yourself.	Lv 19:18
525	4T	. . . fear no evil . . .	Ps 23:4
525	6T	. . . a crown of thorns . . .	Mt 27:29
525	11T	. . . His beloved Son.	Mt 3:17
526	18,19T	. . . every tear is wiped away . . .	Is 25:8
528	14,15T	And if you forgive him his transgressions . . .	Mt 6:12,14
528	18B	Good cannot be returned for evil . . .	Mt 5:44
528	5B	. . . removed it from his own (eyes).	Mt 7:3-5

Page	Lines		Quote	Bible Reference
529		17B	. . . the last trumpet . . .	1 Co 15:52b
529		16B	. . . there is no death.	Rv 21:4b
532		2,1B	. . . eyes have ever seen or ears have heard . . .	Is 64:4
535		2,1B	Be not afraid . . .	Jn 6:20
537		17B	Peace be to you . . .	Jn 20:19, 21a, 26
538	15T		Sin's witnesses . . . call of death.	Rm 6:23
538		20B	The truth is found . . . truth he represents.	Jn 18:37b
539	1,2T		The dying live, the dead arise . . .	Mt 11:5
539		4B	. . . he knows not what he does . . .	Lk 23:34
542		3B	. . . there is no death.	Rv 21:4b
554		5,4B	. . . all the treasures . . . not to thieves . . .	Mt 6:19
555	5T		Be not afraid . . .	Jn 6:20
555	11-23T		The door is open . . . apart from you.	Lk 14:16-23
555	21T		. . . lean years . . .	Gn 41:27
556-57		1B to 1T	. . . for what is joined in Him is always one.	Mt 19:6
557	18T		I thank You, Father . . .	Mt 11:25
558	12,13T		Where fear has gone . . . love must come . . .	1 Jn 4:18
560		4B	. . . "You are beloved of Me . . ."	Mt 3:17
560		4,3B	". . . Be you perfect as Myself . . ."	Mt 5:48

Text (cont'd)

Page	Lines	Quote	Bible Reference
561	16,15B	And what is joined cannot be separate.	Mt 19:6
561	10-8B	Yet who can build his . . . from the wind.	Mt 7:24-27
562	24-7B	It is like the house . . . itself alone.	Mt 7:24-27
562	7B	. . . ark of safety . . .	Gn 7:9
564	5B	"God is Love."	1 Jn 4:8,16
566	2T	. . . the holy ground whereon you stand . . .	Ex 3:5
567	18T	. . . from sickness and from death.	Jn 11:4
568	13,14T	Whom you forgive . . . your illusions.	Mt 16:19b
570-71	1B to 1T	Be very still and hear God's Voice in him . . .	Ps 46:10
571	5T	Behold His Son . . .	Jn 19:5
571	18T	. . . his Father's house.	Jn 14:2
571	20B	. . . how blessed are you . . .	Mt 5:3-11
572	18,19T	He will be as he was and as he is . . .	Heb 13:8
572	7B	. . . only Heaven would not pass away.	Mt 24:35
573	1T	There is no death . . .	Rv 21:4b
573	5T	This world will bind your feet and . . . hands . . .	Jn 11:44
575	9T	. . . there is no death . . .	Rv 21:4b
575	Title et passim	The Anti-Christ	1 Jn 2:18, 22
577	19T	If Heaven is within . . .	Lk 17:21
577	12B	. . . bow down in worship . . . no life.	Ex 32:1-8

Page	Lines		Quote	Bible Reference
577		1B	Judge not . . .	Mt 7:1
578	2T		Judge not . . .	Mt 7:1
578-79		2B to 14T	Seek not to retain the toys . . . put away.	1 Co 13:11
584		12,11B	Whose kingdom is the world for you today?	Mt 6:24
584		1B	And as you have received . . . you give.	Mt 10:8b
585		5B	. . . whom God so loves . . .	Jn 3:16
592	10T	11,2B	. . . look back . . .	Gn 19:26
592		19B	. . . the gate of Heaven . . .	Gn 28:17
592		13B	. . . His Father's house.	Jn 14:2
593	5T		Be merciful . . .	Lk 6:36
594	10T		. . . God is just . . .	Is 45:21
595	19T		"I thank You, Father . . ."	Mt 11:25
595		8,7B	. . . graven image . . .	Ex 20:4
597		14-9B	We have one Interpreter . . . communicate again.	Gn 11:1-9
598		20B	What you ask *is* given you . . .	Mt 7:7a,8a
599	1,2T		And when He has appeared . . . you are like Him . . .	1 Jn 3:2
601	1T		. . . Voice seems small and still . . .	1 K 19:12
601	19T		. . . little Voice, so small and still . . .	1 K 19:12
602		15B	. . . God is Love.	1 Jn 4:8, 16
603	6T		. . . born again . . .	Jn 3:3,7
604		10,9B	Be still and listen.	Ps 46:10
605		17B	He asks and you receive . . .	Mt 7:7a,8a

Text (cont'd)

Page	Lines	Quote	Bible Reference
607	15,14B	For God has said . . . no sacrifice . . . be made.	Ho 6:6
614	10T	You see the flesh or recognize the spirit.	Jn 3:6
615	9,10T	Your will be done! In Heaven . . . true.	Mt 6:10b,c
615	13,14T	. . . "Your will be done."	Mt 6:10b
615	16,15B	. . . forgiven it its trespasses . . .	Mt 6:12,14
615	8,7,4B	Your will . . . Heaven . . . . your will be done!	Mt 6:10b,c
617	20-23T	All things you see . . . nothing with clarity.	1 Co 13:12
620	3,4T	. . . your own weakness . . . Christ in you.	2 Co 12:9b
620	15T	He would not leave you comfortless . . .	Jn 14:18
621	7B	I thank You, Father . . .	Mt 11:25
622	3,2B	. . . everything that lives and moves in You.	Ac 17:28

Page	Lines	Quote	Bible Reference
31	15,16T	And great indeed will be your reward.	Mt 5:12
31	15B	. . . he is the resurrection and the life.	Jn 11:25
31	14B	. . . all power is given . . . Heaven and on earth.	Mt 28:18
59	4T	. . . you have dominion over all things . . .	Gn 1:28
73	4-6T	Those who forgive . . . binding themselves to them.	Mt 16:19b
75	8T	Of yourself you can do none of these things.	Jn 5:19,30
79	2B	Such is the Kingdom of Heaven.	Mt 19:14
86	3B	The images . . . cannot prevail against Him . . .	Mt 16:18
86	2,1B	. . . I will place no other gods before Him.	Ex 20:3
101	Title et passim	"I am the light of the world."	Jn 8:12
101	13B	. . . helps you depart in peace . . .	Lk 2:29
102	3,2B	. . . to build a firm foundation . . .	Lk 6:48
102	2B et. passim	You are the light of the world.	Mt 5:14
103	13-15T	. . . in every attack . . . strength of Christ in you.	2 Co 12:9b
104	2T	How blessed are you . . .	Mt 5:3-11
105	1,2T	"Let me not wander into temptation."	Mt 6:13a
112	2T	This is why you are the light of the world.	Mt 5:14
114	17,18T	. . . those who . . . God in their own image . . . like Himself . . .	Gn 1:26,27

183

Page	Lines	Quote	Bible Reference
116	2T	. . . hiding the light of the world in you.	Mt 5:14
117	13,14T	Then let the power of God work in you . . .	Mt 22:29
117	14,15T	. . . that His Will and yours be done.	Mt 6:10b
120	13,12B	"Seek but do not find."	Mt 7:7b,8b
121	6T	All things are possible to God.	Mt 19:26
124	3T	Ask and you will be answered.	Mt 7:7a,8a
124	3T	Seek and you will find.	Mt 7:7b,8b
126	13,14T	Your will is free, and nothing can prevail against it.	Mt 16:18b
130	10,9B	. . . the glad tidings of your release.	Lk 1:19
135	14,15T	. . . the Kingdom of God is within you . . .	Lk 17:21
143	10,9B	. . . the way, the truth and the life.	Jn 14:6
154	17,16B	For you it is impossible . . . not alone in this.	Mt 19:26
157	19,20T	. . . seen through eyes that cannot see and cannot bless.	Mk 8:18
170	11T	He is with you always, as you are with Him.	Mt 28:20
173	15B	. . . the function . . . on earth as . . . Heaven.	Mt 6:10b,c
174-76	9,8B et passim	God is . . . Love . . .	1 Jn 4:8,16
177	11T	Your joy must be complete . . .	Jn 15:11
182	Title et passim	"God, being Love, is also happiness."	1 Jn 4:8,16
187-88	Title et passim	"Let me be still and listen to the truth."	Ps 46:10

Page	Lines		Quote	Bible Reference
189	6T		From dust to dust they come and go . . .	Gn 2:7
195		9,8B	. . . the truth that comes to set you free.	Jn 8:32
196	5-7T		Let graven images . . . be worshipped not today.	Ex 20:4
196		3,2B	. . . the Word of God that sets you free.	Jn 8:32
196		2B	. . . the key that opens up the gate of Heaven . . .	Mt 16:19a
204	3-5T		*"My function here . . . all the world."*	Mt 16:19b
213		5,4B	As you give you will receive.	Ac 20:35
219		18B	. . . you will see your own transfiguration . . .	Mt 17:2
219		18B	. . . in the glass . . .	1 Co 13:12
220		17,16B	. . . the tidings of salvation . . .	Lk 1:19
221		6B	Only be still and listen.	Ps 46:10
226	19T		. . . He will abide with you . . .	Jn 14:16b
237	17,18T		The sick are healed . . . the dead arise . . .	Mt 10:1,8a
241	7T		. . . the gate of Heaven . . .	Gn 28:17
242		14B	. . . as white as snow.	Is 1:18
243		16B	. . . Heaven's gate.	Gn 28:17
246	3,4T		. . . its (body) value . . . dust and water.	Gn 2:6,7
252	16T		. . . the truth to come and set us free.	Jn 8:32
261	21T		. . . he knows not what he is.	Lk 23:34
263		10B	Peace be to you . . .	Jn 20:19,21a, 26
267	7T		. . . the Lord of Hosts . . .	Ps 46:7,11

Page	Lines		Quote	Bible Reference
272	7,8T		. . . bear false witness to God's Son.	Ex 20:16
272		2B	. . . within the Holy, holy as Itself.	Ex 26:33
273		10,9B	Through your trans-figuration . . . redeemed . . .	Mt 17:2
277		10B	You know not what you do . . .	Lk 23:34
277-78		1B to 2T	Perhaps you will . . . Christ's strength . . . from Him.	2 Co 12:9b
278		12B	God has elected all, but few have come to realize . . .	Mt 20:16b
280	4-7T		We rise up strong in Christ . . . by His strength.	2 Co 12:9b
280		7,6B	Be not afraid nor timid.	Jn 6:20
284	1,2T		There is a way of living . . . seems to be.	Jn 15:19
284		6B	Thus can you serve . . . you serve yourself . . .	Lv 19:18
285	10-12T		. . . accept the truth . . . lighting up the path . . . illusion.	Is 42:16
285	11,12T		. . . ransom from illusion . . . a price.	Ps 49:7
287	11T		Where you are He is.	Jn 14:3
287	12,13T		Nothing can be apart from Him and live.	Ac 17:28
290	9T		. . . Holy One . . .	Ps 16:10
293	17T		The darkened glass the world presents . . .	1 Co 13:12
293		16B	. . . united . . . on earth, as they are one in Heaven.	Mt 6:10b,c
293		8B	. . . and the blind can see.	Mt 11:5

Page	Lines	Quote	Bible Reference
293	5,4B	All can be received but for the asking.	Mt 7:7a,8a
294	8T	. . . holy ground . . .	Ex 3:5
295	18,17B	Is fear His Own, created in His likeness?	Gn 1:26-27
296	12T	Whom God has joined remain forever one . . .	Mt 19:6
296	3,2B	Who denies his brother is denying Him . . .	Mt 25:45
296	2B	. . . the gift of sight . . .	Mk 10:51-52
298	3B	. . . the nails which pierce your own (hands) . . .	Jn 20:25
298	3,2B	. . . lift the crown of thorns . . . bleeding head.	Mt 27:29
300	12,13T	. . . the trumpet of awakening . . . to its call.	Jn 5:25,28-29 1 Co 15:52b
300	14T	And those . . . will never look on death.	Jn 8:51
302-3	Title et passim	"There is no death."	Rv 21:4b
303	6B	*We live and move in You alone.*	Ac 17:28
306	15B	Ask to receive, and it is given you.	Mt 7:7a,8a
311	3T	There is no death . . .	Rv 21:4b
312	7,6B	As we were . . . are . . . will forever be.	Heb 13:8
313	6T	. . . He loves him with a never-changing Love.	Jr 31:3
315	16,15B	. . . bear witness . . . experience of truth . . .	Jn 18:37b
316	3T	. . . bear witness . . .	Jn 18:37b
316	4,5T	. . . this is now at hand.	Mt 3:2
319	17B	. . . gods of vengeance . . .	Rm 12:19

Page	Lines	Quote	Bible Reference
321-27	11B et passim	*"God is but Love . . ."*	1 Jn 4:8,16
322	8B	Hallowed your name.	Mt 6:9
331-33	Title et passim	"I will be still an instant and go home."	Ps 46:10
331	11,10B	. . . His Father's house . . .	Jn 14:2
331	8B	. . . holy ground.	Ex 3:5
334	15-17T	The sick arise . . . blind can see . . . deaf can hear.	Mt 10:1,8a
334	17,18T	The sorrowful . . . tears of pain . . . the world.	Is 25:8
339	10,11T	Many have said . . . few indeed have meant them.	Mt 20:16b
339	13,14T	. . . should any two agree . . .	Mt 18:19
342	6T	. . . the Will of God is done on earth as . . . Heaven.	Mt 6:10b,c
350	13,14T	Is it not He . . . the way to Him.	Jn 14:5
350	17T	Ask and receive.	Mt 7:7a,8a
350	2,1B	*. . . Your Will . . . be done in us . . . part of Heaven now . . .*	Mt 6:10b,c
354	12T	The Son of God has come in glory . . .	Mt 16:27
354	12,13T	. . . to redeem the lost, to save the helpless . . .	Mt 18:11
354	18T	All power is given unto you in . . . Heaven.	Mt 28:18
354	18,19T	There is nothing that you cannot do.	Mt 17:20b
354	6,5B	They must await . . . you are free.	Mt 16:19b
356	11T	Who can be born again in Christ . . .	Jn 3:3,7

Workbook (cont'd)

Page	Lines	Quote	Bible Reference
356	13,12B	Therefore, hold no one prisoner . . . you made free.	Mt 16:19b
358	19B	And He would have all tears wiped away . . .	Is 25:8
358	9B	Give all you can, and give a little more.	Mt 19:21
358	9,8B	. . . arise in haste and go unto our Father's house.	Lk 15:18; Jn 14:2
359	3B	. . . Heaven's gate . . .	Gn 28:17
360	5T	. . . Heaven's gate . . .	Gn 28:17
362	12,11B	It will never be . . . some are . . . bound.	Mt 16:19b
367	9,10T	. . . who know not what their thoughts can do.	Lk 23:34
367	16,17T	The world . . . release from your illusions.	Mt 16:19b
368	8T	. . . for everyone must live and move in Him.	Ac 17:28
370	11B	. . . both on earth and . . . holy home as well.	Mt 6:10
370	11,10B	. . . as you forgive the trespasses . . .	Mt 6:12,14
374	11-9B	You will be bound . . . as he is.	Mt 16:19b
392	Title II	"God is with me. I live and move in Him."	Ac 17:28
401	1,2T	I will arise in glory . . . shine upon the world . . .	Is 60:1
406	10,9B	Let me not think . . . if I have hatred in my heart.	1 Jn 4:20
409	7B	. . . loves him with an everlasting Love . . .	Jr 31:3
409	1B	How long, O holy Son of God, how long?	Ps 89:46

Workbook (cont'd)

Page	Lines		Quote	Bible Reference
412	4T		. . . bear witness to the truth . . .	Jn 18:37b
416	5T		In Him I find my refuge and my strength.	Ps 46:1
417	10T		. . . our Father's house . . .	Jn 14:2
417		12B	*"Father, You stand before me and . . . beside me . . ."*	Ps 139:5
418		5B	This day we enter into paradise . . .	Lk 23:43
425	Lesson 277		"Let me not bind Your Son with laws I made."	Mt 16:19b
434		7B	For God's Will is done in earth and Heaven.	Mt 6:10b,c
434		7,6B	We will seek and we will find . . .	Mt 7:7b,8b
440	Title I		"And God Himself shall wipe away all tears."	Is 25:8
441	Title I		"The holy Christ is born in me today."	Jn 3:3,7
441	7T		. . . is born again in me today.	Jn 3:3,7
445		9B	Be not afraid of love.	Jn 6:20
445		8B	. . . wipe away all tears . . .	Is 25:8
450	Title I		"I came for the salvation of the world."	Jn 18:37a
450		Title II	"My Father gives all power unto me."	Mt 28:18
450		6B	. . . all the strength and love in earth and Heaven.	Mt 28:18
451		6,5B	. . . to let God's Will be done on earth . . .	Mt 6:10b,c
452		6B	. . . Holy One . . .	Ps 16:10

Workbook (cont'd)

Page	Lines	Quote	Bible Reference
453	1T	*"... Your beloved Son ..."*	Mt 3:17
454	7,6B	*And as it is in Heaven, so on earth.*	Mt 6:10b,c
455	Title II	"I choose the second place to gain the first."	Mt 19:30
458	Title II	"Fear binds the world. Forgiveness sets it free."	Mt 16:19b
458	5-3B	*"We would not bind ... release it now."*	Mt 16:19b
461	7B	... His beloved Son ...	Mt 3:17
464	8,7B	... the gate of Heaven ...	Gn 28:17
466	7B	*I would abide in You ...*	Jn 14:16b
467	Title II	"... Your grace suffices me."	2 Co 12:9a
468	7T	Our Father knows our needs.	Mt 6:8
469	5B	... it is written on our hearts.	Rm 2:15
469	4,3B	... glad tidings ...	Lk 1:19
469	16B; 2B	... the gate of Heaven ...	Gn 28:17
470	4B	*You have not left me comfortless.*	Jn 14:18
475	14,13B	He is the way, the truth and life ...	Jn 14:6
475-76	1B to 1T	Or would He rush ... "all I have is his?"	Lk 15:31
477-78	1B to 1T	For we go homeward ... to welcome us.	Lk 15:11-32
478	1B	... I will never leave you comfortless.	Jn 14:18

Manual

Page	Lines		Quote	Bible Reference
3	5T		A light has entered the darkness.	Jn 1:5
3	7,8T		He has become a bringer of salvation.	Lk 1:77
3	12,13T		Many hear It, but few will answer.	Mt 20:16b
5	3T		. . . any two who join together . . .	Mt 18:20
8		10B	. . . governed by a Power . . . *in* them but not *of* them.	Jn 15:19
15		3B	. . . glad tidings . . .	Lk 1:19
15		2B	Blessed indeed are they . . .	Mt 5:3-11
15		2,1B	. . . they are the bringers of salvation.	Lk 1:77
26		12,11B	In order to judge anything rightly . . .	Jn 7:24
36		2B	His Will be done.	Mt 6:10b
37	19,20T		Judge not, for you but judge yourself . . .	Mt 7:1
37		16,15B	Learn to be quiet . . . heard in stillness.	Ps 46:10
37		6,5B	There is no deceit in God.	Is 37:10
37		5B	His promises are sure.	Ps 105:42; Lk 24:49
41	3T		the gate of Heaven . . .	Gn 28:17
44		3B	There is no death.	Rv 21:4b
48		2B	What had been lost has now been found.	Lk 15:24,32
49	1,2T		. . . a kind of peace that is not of this world.	Jn 14:27
51	2,3T		What you ask for you receive.	Mt 7:7a,8a
54		2,1B	"This is my beloved Son . . ."	Mt 3:17

Page	Lines		Quote	Bible Reference
55	4T		The Bible says, "Ask in . . . Jesus Christ."	Jn 14:13,14
55		18B	Remember his promises···	Jn 14:13,14
56		1B	. . . for he is with you; he is always here.	Mt 28:20
60	4,5T		. . . for what is withheld from love is given to fear . . .	1 Jn 4:18
61	3T		. . . His Word is written on everyone's heart.	Rm 2:15
64	10T		"And the last to be overcome will be death."	1 Co 15:26
67		5B	"Of myself I can do nothing" . . .	Jn 5:19,30
68		19,18B	For God has given Him . . . His language.	Rm 8:26
68		15-12B	A loving father . . . Father love His Son?	Mt 7:9-11
68		11,10B	Remember your weakness is His strength.	2 Co 12:9
69	9T		. . . of all things visible . . .	Col 1:16
79	14,15T		God knows what His Son needs before he asks.	Mt 6:8
79		17,16B	He is as . . . from this gate . . .	Gn 28:17
82		4,3B	Hallowed your name and His . . .	Mt 6:9
83	7T		Their names are legion . . .	Mk 5:9
84		6B	*"There is no death . . ."*	Rv 21:4b
85	1,2T		Jesus . . . Holy Spirit . . . ascended into Heaven . . .	Ac 1:8,9
85	5T		. . . in His likeness or spirit . . .	Gn 1:26,27

Page	Lines		Quote	Bible Reference
85	16T		All power in Heaven and earth is . . . given him . . .	Mt 28:18
85		4B	. . . a far country . . .	Lk 15:13
87	11T		. . . the Holy of Holies . . .	Ex 26:33
87	13,14T		. . . loves you as He loves Himself.	Lv 19:18
87	14T		Ask but my help to roll the stone away . . .	Mt 28:2
87	19T		Be not afraid.	Jn 6:20
87		1B	. . . morning star . . .	Rv 2:28

B. Bible
1. Old Testament
2. New Testament

Old Testament
Genesis

Exodus

Leviticus

Numbers

Deuteronomy

Judges

1 Kings

Job

Chapter & Verses	Book	Page	Lines
2:9	T	. . .471	.14B . . . .
13:9 (see Ga 6:7a)		. . . .	. . . .
19:25	T	. . .194	.20T . . . .
19:25	T	. . .204	.8B . . . .

Psalms

Psalms (cont'd)

Psalms (cont'd)

Proverbs

Ecclesiastes

Isaiah

Jeremiah

Ezekiel

Daniel

Hosea

Chapter & Verses	Book	Page	Lines

2:1 (see 1 Co 15:52b) . . . .

New Testament
Matthew

Matthew (cont'd)

Matthew (cont'd)

Matthew (cont'd)

Chapter & Verses	Book	Page	Lines
19:6	T	139	10,9B
19:6	T	332	17T
19:6	T	435	1,2T
19:6	T	446	13,14T
19:6	T	517-18	1B to 1T
19:6	T	556-57	1B to 1T
19:6	T	561	15,16T
19:6	W	296	12T
19:14	T	75	19B
19:14	W	79	2B
19:18 (see Ex 20:16)			
19:19 (see Lv 19:18)			
19:21	T	205	13T
19:21	W	358	9B
19:26	T	194	10,9B
19:26	W	121	6T
19:26	W	154	17,16B
19:30 (20:16a)	W	455	Title II

Chapter & Verses	Book	Page	Lines
20:16a (see 19:30)			
20:16b (22:14)	T	39	17T
20:16b (22:14)	W	278	12B
20:16b (22:14)	W	339	10,11T
20:16b (22:14)	M	3	12,13T
20:19	T	395	13T
20:28 (see Ps 49:7)			

Chapter & Verses	Book	Page	Lines
21:9 (see Ps 118:26)			
21:13 (see Jr 7:11)			
21:22	T	152	2B

Matthew (cont'd)

Mark

Luke

Luke (cont'd)

Chapter & Verses	Book	Page	Lines
11:36	T	185	16B
14:16-23	T	555	11-23T
15:7	T	225	16,17T
15:7	T	244	14T
15:7	T	511	1,2T
15:11-32	T	138	14-21T
15:13	M	85	4B
15:18	W	358	9,8B
15:20	W	477-78	1B to 1T
15:24,32	T	395	16T
15:24,32	M	48	2B
15:31	T	193	11B
15:31	W	475-76	1B to 1T
16:8 (see 1 Th 5:5)			
17:21	T	54	18,17B
17:21	T	197	21,20B
17:21	T	287	18T
17:21	T	293	2T
17:21	T	490	20T
17:21	T	577	19T
17:21	W	135	14,15T
21:23 (see Jn 3:36)			

John

John (cont'd)

Acts

Chapter & Verses	Book	Page	Lines
1:8 (Is 43:10,12)	T ...	9	.... 12B ....
1:8,9 (2:1-4)	M ...	85	.... 1,2T ....

2:1-4 (see 1:8,9) ....

17:28	T ...	110	.... 5,4B ....
17:28	T ...	476	.... 15,14B ......
17:28	T ...	622	.... 3,2B ....
17:28	W ...	287	.... 12,13T ....
17:28	W ...	303	.... 6B ....
17:28	W ...	368	.... 8T ....
17:28	W ...	392	.... Title II ......

20:35	T ...	2	.... 11,12T ....
20:35	T ...	430	.... 6,7T ....
20:35	W ...	213	.... 5,4B ....

1 Corinthians

2 Corinthians

Ephesians

Philippians

Colossians

1 Thessalonians

1 Timothy

Chapter & Verses	Book	Page	Lines
6:16 (see Rv 5:12,13)			

2 Timothy

Hebrews

1 John

Revelation